The Persuasion Explosion

Art Stevens

The Persuasion Explosion

Your Guide to the Power & Influence of Contemporary Public Relations

ACROPOLIS BOOKS LTD.

WASHINGTON, D.C.

To Eva, my wife.
To Amelia, my partner.

ACROPOLIS BOOKS LTD.
Colortone Building, 2400 17th St., N.W.
Washington, D.C. 20009

Printed in the United States of America by
COLORTONE PRESS
Creative Graphics, Inc.
Washington, D.C. 20009

Library of Congress Cataloging in Publication Data
Stevens, Art, 1935-
    The persuasion explosion
    1. Public relations—United States. 2. Publicity—United States. I. Title.
HM263.S865 1985   659.2'0973   85-6238
ISBN 0-87491-732-8

CONTENTS

Foreword
9

FOREWORD

"Persuade—to cause someone to do something by means of advice, reasoning, or entreaty; to win over someone to a course of action by reasoning or inducement."

"Explosion—a sudden and great increase."

When these dictionary definitions of the two elements in the title of this book are put together, they conjure up yet another definition: mine.

The "Persuasion Explosion"—a uniquely American phenomenon reflecting the proliferating number of products, services, causes, and issues in our lives and the vast means by which we win people over to them.

A number of books have been written on the enormous powers of advertising as a "persuader." Yet another singularly American communications tool—public relations—may arguably be even more powerful and pervasive than advertising.

Although public relations is at the heart of the persuasion explosion, it is little understood by those not in direct contact with its practice. Yet it touches us all in one way or another.

The field of public relations has expanded exponentially in both the number of practitioners and the range of their involvement in all facets of society—corporate, social, civic, political, academic, and even religious.

While at the outset publicity comprised the bulk of the public relations professional's work, the field has evolved through the years to encompass a broad range of skills important to management of any enterprise but not generally found in executives trained in other specialties and professions.

The practice of public relations was pioneered at the beginning of this century by such brilliant practitioners as the late Ivy Lee and Edward L. Bernays (at 93 still its outstanding champion), but the persuasion explosion is a phenomenon of the past 40 or so years.

No single volume could fully cover either the history or the excitement of the persuasion explosion. The aim of this book is rather to familiarize you, the reader, with a powerful, dominant force that affects us all; to share some insights on what public relations is; to acquaint you with public relations people, strategies, and anecdotes; and, finally, to show you how to borrow public relations techniques from the professionals to enrich your business and personal life.

I love public relations. It's a stimulating, roller-coastering, chest-beating, humbling, hair-pulling, all-encompassing field. Come along for the ride and see if you want to get off.

Art Stevens

CHAPTER ONE

A UNIVERSAL CRAFT

Let's start with what public relations is not.

A beautiful young woman runs an ad in a magazine accompanied by a photograph of her in a bikini. The ad says: "Attention, Meeting & Convention Planners. I can be your public relations representative at your next event." This is not public relations.

A lonely senior citizen calls a travel agency and tells the travel agent that she plans a month's vacation to Europe and seeks a "public relations escort" to accompany her. This is not public relations.

Not long ago I was sitting in a restaurant nibbling on a sandwich. It was dry. I asked the waitress to bring me some mayonnaise on the side. She did. I thanked her. She said, "Think nothing of it. I just practice good public relations." This is not public relations.

A Mafia chief instructs one of his lieutenants on the art of collecting protection money from neighborhood stores. "If they go two, three times without coughing up the dough, throw a rock through the window. If they don't pay by the fifth time, rough them up. That's Mafia public relations."

This is not public relations.

Let's talk about what public relations *is*.

Public relations is a universal craft.

What we think depends largely on what we perceive and how we perceive it. We are constantly trying to alter the opinions of others, at work and in our personal lives. We are constantly exposed to information about people, ideas, products, and services, beamed at us with the intention of influencing our perceptions. Everyone practices public relations, naturally and instinctively. People from all segments of society use public relations approaches in community work and similar enterprises. Some are good at it. Many are not; not because they lack the necessary instincts, but because they are amateurs in a field calling for professionals.

At the professional level, public relations people use their skills to persuade the public as to products, services, issues, and people. As in all professional endeavors, some professionals are good at it, some are not.

I'm a public relations professional in what is actually a craft rather than a discrete profession. I've been successful at my craft. I'd like to think that's because I'm good at what I do, and that I understand the dynamics of persuasion and perception. Like my colleagues in the field, I have worked long and hard to master the right skills.

At the same time, I am deeply aware of the responsibilities that go with the job. The true public relations professional can unleash and direct powerful forces. The greater the command of PR skills, the greater the need for an ethical compass in good working order.

The field's high potential for good (or bad) helps to account for the extremes of public reaction it often generates. Public relations is maligned and attacked the most by two disparate groups of people: those who know virtually nothing about it, and those who work with it most closely—the media. Those who decry public relations say it is slick, glossy, misleading, deceptive, and damaging. Good public relations is none of these.

But nobody says it is ineffective. Everyone who understands what public relations is—friend or foe—acknowledges its power.

One of the accusations that has been directed at PR professionals is that, like lawyers, we sometimes represent unpopular causes or "bad" people. But it is inaccurate to equate public relations with the legal profession. Attorneys do represent individuals who are less than exemplary citizens. It is the ethical nature of the lawyer's responsibility that legal representation be given to everyone. The same cannot be said of public relations.

There is no similar constitutional right to be represented by public relations counsel. In fact, the reputable practitioner will represent a client only if his cause—whether issue, product, or service—is consistent with the public interest. Others, like Edward L. Bernays, the venerable dean of the craft, will not represent a client whose cause they do not believe in.

As Amanda Brown-Olmstead, president of A. Brown-Olmstead Associates, a leading Atlantic public relations firm, puts it: "I would never represent a client who is running a dishonest business, who is not credit-worthy, or whose approach to business is morally questionable.

"I would also not take business that represents an issue I do not believe in. For example, I turned down a political candidate who spoke out against the Equal Rights Amendment."

Neil Amidei, president of the San Francisco-based public relations firm Hoefer-Amidei, will not take cigarette accounts, or represent any group that advocates the proliferation of nuclear weapons.

"But," he points out, "it would be a challenge to represent a company that may have done something wrong, like a chemical company that polluted a body of water, and is now attempting to right that wrong. I could enthusiastically embark on such a program."

Another criticism is that public relations is heartless—that it is devoted to advancing the selfish aims of clients. This is very wide of the mark. Public relations does in fact serve, in a significant way, as the social conscience of corporate America.

The public relations profession is a 20th-century phenomenon. But its roots go back to 1791 and the adoption of the First Amendment to the Constitution of the United States:

Congress shall make no law respecting an establishment of religion, or prohibiting the free exercise thereof; *or abridging the freedom of speech, or of the press;* or the right of the people peaceably to assemble, and to petition the Government for a redress of grievances.

The guarantee of free speech and a free press is basic to a democratic society. With this freedom (a rarity in the world of that era) people were given the opportunity to persuade others by telling their stories through the media—or on the stump—without fear of being silenced.

It's not surprising, then, that public relations as a profession began in the United States. It is rooted in our traditions.

Our country is blessed by the freedom given to people from all walks of life to try to effect change by persuading others through their own direct efforts. In a sense this book is designed to enhance, to some degree, our use of this magnificent opportunity by helping more people to understand and use the principles and techniques of persuasion. Everyone can participate in the persuasion explosion in one way or another.

Charles Darwin's theory of evolution by natural selection in the mid-19th century aroused tumultuous debate and ferocious opposition. Biologist Darwin, introspective and reclusive, was totally unsuited to the task of trying to persuade scientists, churchmen, and the general public to consider—let alone accept—his theory. But when naturalist Thomas Henry Huxley assumed the role of Darwin's defender, he orchestrated a campaign that led to broad acceptance of the highly controversial theory of evolution in an astonishingly short time. His was a public relations feat.

French General Henri Philippe Pétain became a symbol of the indomitability of France during the darkest days of World

War I. Marshal Pétain's status as a national hero led to his being installed as the head of the Vichy government when the Germans conquered France in World War II. The general's collaboration with the Nazis led to his eventual conviction and imprisonment as a traitor. Now it is known that, even as this bluff, earthy soldier was leading France's armies at the battle of Verdun in 1916, he had a team of public relations specialists working at headquarters. They were particularly skilled at placing stories in the American newspapers, to be picked up in turn by the French press.

Pétain's reputation as a heroic military leader, which he so adroitly enhanced, led ultimately to disaster for him and for France in what was later revealed as a glaring example of the inappropriate use of image-building skills.

An example such as this fuels the fires of those who attack public relations. But they miss the point. Public relations, unfortunately, can be used for good or for bad. It is today's equivalent of the genie of the Arabian Nights who, when freed from its bottle, worked miracles that shook the earth. The direction taken by the forces of persuasion when they are unleashed depends on the objectives and integrity of the practitioner and his client.

The once-secret role of the public relations specialist in various areas is now acknowledged openly. In politics, for example. Not so long ago it was widely assumed that candidates and political and business leaders wrote their own speeches, or even made them up as they went along—and that spectacular events like the "kitchen debate" between Richard Nixon and Nikita Khrushchev just happened by chance. Now we know better. We know, for example, that the confrontation in the Moscow kitchen display that added so much luster to Nixon's reputation was shaped by Bill Safire, my mentor, friend, and former boss.

We now see lively and open discussion on who is writing the president's speeches, and which public relations specialists are working for him at the moment. Indeed, the choice of a

PR director becomes, in itself, a significant political event. The situation has developed so that people in the media set considerable store by which of several candidates political mastermind David Garth chooses to work for. Garth, a New York-based public relations professional, specializes in running campaigns for political candidates. His reputation has been established as a result of his backing many more winners than losers. Mr. Garth's skill as a master of political public relations is such that the mere fact that he elects to work for candidate Smith instead of candidate Jones may move Smith up in the polls, at least temporarily.

The role of PR in legal matters—often an important consideration for lawyers—has grown significantly in recent years. Attorneys for one-time automotive tycoon John DeLorean held almost daily press conferences on the courthouse steps to drive home their contention that he had been entrapped into participating in a drug deal with undercover agents. In the closely watched and highly significant libel suit filed by General William Westmoreland against CBS (over what was claimed to be the network's libelous depiction of the general's alleged manipulation of figures on North Vietnamese military strength, shown on *Sixty Minutes*), the opposing forces employed public relations counsel who operated as openly as legal counsel, providing information to the media and striving to put their viewpoints across. As Professor Geoffrey Hazard, of the Yale Law School, observed, "Both sides are seeking a public opinion verdict as well as a jury verdict."

And that's what it's all about—in marketing, in politics, in entertainment, and now in the law and practically every other major area of human endeavor: seeking a *favorable* public opinion verdict.

Winning favorable verdicts in the court of public opinion normally is the work of the PR practitioner. I'm proud of my record of victories in this "court." But there's more to it than the joy of winning. There's the exhilaration of using powerful tools to achieve positive ends; the never-ending interest that lies in meeting new challenges, turning public apathy into interest, making "dull" things fascinating; and the sheer fun of being in a field that involves me with the matchlessly entertaining observation and understanding of human behavior, individually and en masse.

Public relations is a paradoxical craft. Unlike such professions as neurosurgery, law, accounting, and architecture, it is practiced by persons who often are specialists in a wide variety of fields. One finds graduates in law, journalism, writing, engineering, and other disciplines pursuing careers as public relations practitioners. Partially because of this, and although practically everyone knows about PR, there is vast misunderstanding about its real nature. Some people think it's the same as advertising. Others think it's being a press agent. Still others have a vague idea that public relations means "being nice to people."

Above all, people have come to think of PR as the manipulation of image.

PR thus has an image problem of its own. For despite popular titles like *The Image Merchants*, and catch phrases like "the image society," public relations is *not* the art of creating a fictitious image and passing it off as truth. "Image," in that sense, is created by emotion. Public relations instead deals with *perception*, which means awareness, understanding, comprehension. Perception is created and shaped by information.

At this point it's time for a definition.

Public Relations News, a weekly newsletter written for the PR profession, defines public relations as a management function that evaluates public attitudes, identifies the policies and procedures of an individual or an organization as they affect the public interest, and executes a program of action to earn public understanding and acceptance. Implicit in this definition is the function of the professional public relations expert, which is threefold: to ascertain and evaluate public opinion, to counsel management on ways of dealing with public opinion as it exists, and to use communications to influence public opinion.

I have my own definition:

Public relations
is the shaping of perception,
through communication,
for the achievement of positive goals.

Shaping perception may mean creating a perception, maintaining one, or revising one. *Communication* covers the array of tools and techniques used to influence perception. The emphasis on *positive* goals means that the power of public relations must be used decently, responsibly, and with the highest regard for legal and ethical standards.

The PR professional, then, is essentially a specialist in communications. His or her goal is to make you take a course of action—to buy a product, to vote for a candidate, to contribute to a charity, to take public transportation, to support or oppose a cause, to go to church, or to go out on strike. I could add thousands of activities to this list.

According to Scott Cutlip and Allen H. Center, authors of *Effective Public Relations*, PR is often confused with its functional parts—for example, publicity, institutional advertising, product promotion, and lobbying. The field with which public relations is most often confused by the public is advertising. There's a big difference. Advertising pays for print space or air time in order to sell a specific product or issue, while public relations, which may utilize some forms of advertising as a tool, is much broader in scope—and generally utilizes a mix of tools other than paid space and time.

Public relations makes use of such communications techniques as news and feature stories, guests on radio and television talk shows, slide films, speeches, booklets and brochures, photographs, exhibits, displays, employee publications, press conferences, radio and television scripts, and stockholder reports.

A public relations person may be the vice president of a large corporation or a publicist for a small community group. People like Ron Ziegler, Bill Moyers, Pierre Salinger, and Jody

Powell performed the tasks for Presidents of the United States that their counterparts in industry perform for captains of industry.

The public relations function may be handled by internal staff members or by outside agencies. A PR department within a company may consist of one person or several hundred. The larger the staff, the more specialized the work of each staff member. One individual may write and edit an employee newsletter, another person may write speeches for key executives, another may organize and conduct plant tours or write news stories on specific products, and yet another may handle dealings with the financial community. What the public relations department is called—for example, News Bureau, Public Affairs, Corporate Communications, Publicity Department, or Issue Management—varies from company to company.

A company with a public relations department may retain an agency as an additional arm. If there is no public relations department, the agency functions as the sole PR voice. Firms are hired either on a yearly retainer basis or on a special project basis—and sometimes consultants are retained for advice.

The objectives of public relations are diverse. The swelling memberships of such professional organizations as the Public Relations Society of America and the International Association of Business Communicators are a clear indication that although many may not understand public relations, more and more are beginning to use it.

A breakdown of U.S. organizations that report using public relations includes corporations, public utilities, transportation companies, banks, trade and professional associations, educational institutions, hospitals, government in its many forms, foundations, health and welfare agencies and citizen groups.

The problems for public relations in government are considerably different from those in business and industry. For example, the major problem facing a press secretary to a highly visible figure like Mayor Edward Koch of New York City is how to make the public aware of the important but less glamorous activities of the Mayor's Office.

"During a crisis or emergency," says one of the Mayor's press representatives, "we have no problem getting news coverage of the Mayor's position. Our problem is getting press interests in matters that are far less dramatic, but that deserve public awareness anyway. For example, in New York City, some great inroads have been made in environmental protection—air pollution control, sanitation, water protection. But the public isn't as aware of these solid but undramatic stories as it is of the crises that dominate the headlines.

"Our primary function is to act as a channel between City Hall and the people of New York City. The service we provide is making understandable how government functions."

St. Clair T. Bourne, former executive assistant to the Commissioner of the New York State Division of Housing, holds a similar view on the problems of government public relations. "The greatest difference between government public relations and its counterpart in business," he says, "is that our stockholders are the public, which is paying for the cost of government services. Government policies, regulations, and activities are often complex. Our task is to facilitate understanding of complicated matters."

In many ways, the basic skills needed in conducting a political campaign are no different from those needed to sell a product. This fact was evident in recent presidential campaigns in which both candidates made extensive use of all available communication tools.

In the area of business-financial public relations, a PR agency often is called in by an emerging corporation that is flexing its new corporate muscles, particularly if the company is selling stock to the public for the first time. Companies that are unknown are anxious for public awareness of their products and growth potential—and the attendant desirability of their shares.

The public relations effort for these growing companies focuses on ways of giving them national recognition—for example, interviews with business and financial newspapers and magazines for the company's executives, annual and quarterly reports for stockholders, meetings with security analysts, and news releases on corporate activities.

Public relations activities of publicly held companies are under constant scrutiny by the Securities and Exchange Commission and the stock exchanges. Questionable practices like stock touting, delayed disclosure of corporate news to allow insiders to purchase stock before it's available to the public, misrepresentation and doctoring balance sheets to distort the true financial position of a company are all dealt with severely.

It is generally the fly-by-night corporation in collusion with a dishonest public relations practitioner or firm that engages in such practices. Most companies would rather settle for a fair stock price that accurately reflects the company's current position. And most public relations firms, like companies in any other field, find that proper ethical conduct is by far the wisest and most rewarding policy.

The New York Stock Exchange stands at the heart of a multibillion dollar service industry. The Exchange provides a marketplace in which millions of individual investors—and financial institutions that represent half of the U.S. population—buy and sell ownership shares of most of America's leading corporations. Eugene Miller, a former vice-president for public relations and investor services of the Exchange, points out that while its primary function is to run an efficient securities marketplace that attracts and merits the confidence of the investing public, "a major corollary function is to keep the public promptly and accurately informed about what happens in the market—and the policies and techniques that are developed to keep the market running smoothly." "This, in turn," he says, "requires a major educational effort to provide the necessary background for understanding, interpreting, and participating in the investment process."

These views are a far cry from the attitude of big business at the turn of the century, when concern for the public good often was a negligible factor in corporate decision-making. In those days, the maxim of some was "The public be damned."

This attitude has since undergone a complete turnabout but

many corporate executives remain at a loss as to how to interpret and evaluate the impact of public opinion on the activities of their companies. They may be experts on manufacturing schedules, research and development procedures, mergers and acquisitions, and marketing, but when it comes to PR, they're often in unfamiliar territory.

As is the case with advertising, an individual needs no special license to practice public relations. The Public Relations Society of America has, however, established a program to raise professional standards and to improve the practice of public relations. Implicit in these standards is the recognition that the communications techniques, public perceptions, and sociological changes that characterize our rapidly changing, technologically oriented society demand greater knowledge and skills of public relations people than ever before.

Can public relations results be measured? By and large, yes: A candidate gets elected, a budding actor gets his picture in the newspaper, a company's community relations problem is solved, or a new product wins immediate recognition. Often results are measured in terms of the extent to which a favorable attitude toward an individual or organization can be created in a specific market or audience.

Edward L. Bernays, at 93 the elder statesman of the public relations field, tells the story of his long-time client Procter & Gamble and the concern the company felt many years ago over the perception young children had of soap.

It seems that the company's research had determined that young children could grow up to hate soap because when it got in their eyes it would sting and be mildly painful. Procter & Gamble officials were worried that this new generation of Americans might grow up hating soap so much that the market share for their products would decline dramatically. They asked Bernays what could be done.

Bernays, doing further research into the habit and interests of children, concluded that their creative instincts could be nurtured early on to create future positive reinforcement: if he could get children to play with soap in a creative way, they would grow up with more positive attitudes toward it.

Putting his conviction to work, Bernays created a national soap sculpture program for Procter & Gamble. In one year he had 22 million children carve artistic objects out of Ivory Soap, helping to create a lasting marketplace for that venerable product.

As Bernays has always put it, public relations is more action than words.

In another example of Bernays' brilliance, he got an entire nation to add bacon to its breakfast regimen—on behalf of, you guessed it, a bacon manufacturer. Most of us grew up on bacon and eggs. But in the 1920's, when Bernays was putting his stamp on the newly founded public relations profession, most Americans were breakfasting on bread and coffee. A bacon company, appealing to his considerable resourcefulness and creativity, asked him to help put bacon on the breakfast table.

Bernays began his assignment with his own physician. He asked the good doctor whether a heavy morning meal was better nutritionally than a light one. The physician thought about it and allowed as how a heavy breakfast might well start the day off better than a light breakfast.

Using this opinion as his starting point, Bernays engaged the services of a scientific data service to poll some 5,000 physicians throughout the country, asking the same basic question. The vast majority of the respondees ventured the medical opinion that yes, a substantial breakfast was better, and that, yes, bacon and eggs would indeed be a good way to start the day off with a nutritional meal.

Once these findings were released to the newspapers, it wasn't long before Americans' breakfast habits began to change. Bacon was on its way to becoming the breakfast king.

In an age of specialization, many PR professionals become experts in particular areas—for example, government, politics, corporate finance, or labor relations. Within specific industries, public relations people often specialize in complex and technical subjects in order to present them in readily understandable terms. But a new role for the generalist is also emerging.

Within the next 10 years, a new breed of executive can be expected to enter the field of business communications. This new breed will consist of generalists rather than specialists. They will know something about everything that comes under the heads of advertising, public relations, product publicity, labor relations, community relations, or stockholder information services.

But these new generalists will know less about any one of these areas than the specialists that work under them. Just as today's auto company president knows far less about design than his chief of design and a steel company president leaves the details of production to his chief of production, so our manager will be a generalist rather than a specialist. He or she will, however, know more than any one specialist about how to mesh the specialties harmoniously.

We had better get to know these new generalists, because they are the men and women who will lead the public relations business across the frontiers of tomorrow.

Public relations, as a craft, has come of age. It attracts top people, counsels thousands of corporations and organizations, makes use of sophisticated communications techniques, and is deeply involved in almost every phase of contemporary life. Through the profession's own efforts, public relations standards of performance are at a peak. Yesterday's PR man has been relegated to mythology; he is no longer representative of today's reality. Public relations, 1980's style, has become an integral part of American know-how.

In our western culture, public relations exists as a growing and vital profession because we live in an open and democratic society and because we have freedom of speech and of the press. Because of this all viewpoints can be expressed and conveyed to the public. The gathering of news has become an enormous undertaking by the media. There are simply not enough reporters to effectively cover all of the newsworthy events that take place on any given day.

Enter public relations. Public relations naturally takes an advocacy role in presenting the views of its clients and constituents. The media recognizes this. Nevertheless, the media must make use of public relations professionals to provide news and views on a vast variety of current topics. Their once-grudging acceptance of public relations has now given way to a relative willingness to use its services.

Public relations is a positive force in our society because it assists in the presentation of all points of view—freedom of speech and of the press is a central tenet of an open society. Many crises involving the public denunciation of organizations and institutions by the media could be averted if these organizations and institutions consistently practiced the elements of good public relations—honesty, openness and candor. Corporations that are perceived as devious by the media are likely to be treated poorly. By the same token, the media respect forthrightness in those who are in the news, or who create the news, and will bend over backward to be fair. There is a quid pro quo in the relationship between the media and public relations professionals.

My young niece once asked me why she didn't read about the growth of public relations in her history books. Perhaps one day she will, when public relations takes its rightful place among the world's most powerful professions. As a profession, it represents virtually all of the others before the public. As a profession, it raises the level of communications between individuals and groups. Public relations people can—and do— make a tremendous difference in contemporary society. I exhort them to rise to their fullest powers and potential as communicators, conveyors, and developers of points of view, and counselors to those seeking to communicate more effectively.

Public relations is not about telling untruths because the boss wants it that way. It's about persuading, informing, educating, and influencing. It's about helping you make up your mind on any number of matters. It's about being the most powerful communications force in the world today.

The pages that follow are designed to help you use the power of PR to turn your goals—personal and professional— into reality. Because today's persuasion explosion touches your life in every way.

The power of persuasion changed John D. Rockefeller's reputation from tyrannical business tycoon to kindly, benevolent old man in an historic "first" for the emerging field of U.S. public relations.

CHAPTER TWO

RX FOR A PROFESSIONAL INFERIORITY COMPLEX

For many years public relations people suffered from a group inferiority complex. They were defensive about their craft. Typically, a PR professional would be the first in a gathering to tell the latest derogatory joke about "flacks" and to denigrate the discipline.

This is no longer the case. Public relations professionals now feel far more positive and confident about their vocation. And it's not just because they're paid better salaries and rank higher on the corporate ladder, or because PR now attracts more bright, well-trained and responsible people than it once did. These factors are important, but the change in outlook of public relations practitioners also reflects some important changes in the way we see ourselves as a society.

A closer look at those changes offers, I believe, some useful insights.

In a study I conducted about 10 years ago for *Public Relations Quarterly*, I asked more than 800 public relations professionals to rate themselves in a list of nine professions. Included were medicine, science, law, business, writing, music, government, art, and public relations. Of the nine professions, public relations professionals rated themselves dead last. The public relations professionals who responded to this study judged medicine the number one occupation, followed by science, law, business, writing, music, government, art, and public relations.

Thus, 10 years ago, despite their protestations to the contrary, public relations professionals still thought of themselves as second-class professional citizens. For example, although an overwhelming 82 percent contended that public relations had made less progress in terms of professional image than other professions, an equally whopping 84 percent found their profession to be from "somewhat" to "extremely" satisfying.

When asked whether, if they had it to do over, they would choose public relations as a profession, 65 percent said yes. And 71 percent said yes, that given the option, they would stay in public relations.

Yet 74 percent thought that public relations did not attract the best people, and 84 percent that public relations did not have a good image. An incredible 98 percent felt that most people do not understand what public relations is.

In further confirmation of the negative views PR people then believed outsiders had of their profession, 78 percent of those surveyed felt that they were accorded less respect than members of other professions. (Shades of Rodney Dangerfield.)

One of the primary reasons public relations people in years past were so defensive is that the media tended to be so destructively critical of public relations. Public relations people began to believe what they heard and read in the media.

In those days, however, the media usually were regarded as highly objective forces. Since then we have become more sophisticated about newspapers, magazines, television, and radio. We're well aware that they don't simply report the news; they *shape* it—by means of emphasis, slant, and omission. They also *create* news; in the 1984 presidential election Ronald

Reagan's age was virtually a nonissue until the *Wall Street Journal* carried a lead story about it. And they influence the way we think about the news. Two candidates debate. Those watching and listening, according to polls taken immediately afterward, find it a tie. Then television and radio commentators announce that candidate A has won decisively. Polls taken three days later show that the public now agrees that A won decisively.

And the media are not exactly immune to manipulation. Far from it. A generation of terrorists, including the captors of the Americans at the U.S. Embassy in Teheran, has demonstrated that it is not difficult to get on national TV and plead their cause—to have what they say covered not as editorial comment, but as news.

The media have learned some sobering things about themselves. They have become somewhat less quick to assault public relations. And public relations professionals, in turn, are learning that the true relationship between media and PR is one of mutual dependency. There is far too much going on in the world for the media to cover alone. The press must rely on responsible PR professionals to provide important information. Obviously such information is provided with a purpose. But if it is interesting, factual, and useful, it is news. In the past, public relations never really won the "good press" for itself that it did for its clients and constituencies, but today things are different. My conversations with hundreds of public relations practitioners throughout the country make it clear that the perception of public relations has changed rapidly. As a result the field now attracts more bright and responsible individuals. Indeed, there is a shortage of highly qualified public relations professionals today, and salaries for corporate public relations senior managers range up to $250,000 to $300,000. Top management of Fortune 1,000 companies select their public relations managers more carefully than ever before and often with the assistance of top-ranked executive recruiting firms.

The new breed of public relations practitioner exhibits more self-confidence, and insists upon and gets greater respect from colleagues in other professions.

The corporation has traditionally been viewed as a cold, soulless entity, interested only in profit. And, right or wrong, businesses tended to act this way in the 19th and early 20th century. Today, however, corporations are extensively involved in acts of good will and public concern: supporting the arts, serving the community, helping the unfortunate. It would be hard to find a major U.S. company that is not involved in one or more public service activities. Typical examples include the Texaco Philanthropic Foundation's aid to hospitals and colleges; Eagle Rare Bourbon's campaign to preserve the American bald eagle; the Colgate Women's Games; Pepsi Cola's collaboration with the State University of New York to turn the company's Purchase, N.Y., headquarters into an important cultural center; Mutual Benefit Life's deep involvement in Renaissance Newark, a program to revitalize the company's headquarters city; Champion International's collaboration with the Whitney Museum; and Hertz's Number One awards for high school athletes.

Companies of all kinds are doing marvelous things for their communities and the country. Public relations is the catalyst for these activities. They are not undertaken by accident; they are undertaken to create a more favorable perception of the company. They achieve this at the same time they do immense good for society, and this is something we in PR are proud of.

We're also proud of the wealth of opportunities PR provides for professionals of both sexes. An outstanding example of women's achievements in the field is Tina Santi Flaherty, now Senior Vice President for Corporate Communications at GTE, who is one of the most respected and highest paid PR executives in the country. Before going to GTE she held a similar post at Colgate Palmolive, where she created the Colgate Women's Games, which gives hundreds of underprivileged youngsters throughout the United States the opportunity to participate in athletic competition. She says, "I'm pleased to say that GTE pursued me, not because I am a woman, but because the company felt I am a talented and capable public relations professional. While the floodgates have not fully opened at the corporate level, I like to feel that what I have achieved can serve as an example for women throughout the country."

According to Jack O'Dwyer, editor and publisher of Jack O'Dwyer's Newsletter, a weekly newsletter covering the public relations field, more and more women are becoming owners of major public relations agencies or top executives of Fortune 500 companies.

"As I monitor events that have a bearing on the public relations field," he says, "I notice that there are more women than men taking communications and public relations courses in colleges and universities. And they are encouraged by professors who are quick to point out the limitless opportunities for women in the field. Interestingly, because of this trend, there are also some fine opportunities for men, who are beginning to be seen as a minority group, particularly at the agency level."

The professionalism of the media has also risen dramatically. Many business reporters, writers, and editors are MBAS. They bring to their craft greater knowledge and greater abilities. Often in the old days, all you had to do to get a story into a newspaper was wine and dine a reporter. He would see to it that your company or your client's article appeared in the morning edition. Several high-level business writers were reputed to have tables available for them on a daily basis at major restaurants; if they were called by a public relations person early enough during the day, that person would have the "privilege" of having lunch with the editor, paying for it, and selling an article about a client. It is small wonder that the fields of journalism and public relations tended to disparage each other. Public relations people would poke fun at the life-support systems being offered to them by reporters on the take. And reporters in turn would call their public relations colleagues "hacks" because all public relations people wanted to do was buy them lunch and sell them a story.

The wining and dining relationship between the media and public relations has largely come to an end. Reporters, writers, and editors are much too busy to spend valuable time being wined and dined. In fact, many of them dislike using the business lunch as a means to discuss clients and organizations. The relationship has become much more professional. The fact that today's public relations people are far more sophisticated and knowledgeable about the needs of the media than some of the "hacks" of the past has heightened media respect for the professionalism of the public relations field. As a whole, the give and take between the two has thus become more businesslike in recent years. The alliance between the two fields may still be a bit uneasy but it is clear that one cannot function without the other and a new mutual respect is evolving.

Question: What do a corporate board chairman, a nurse, a PTA president, and a union leader have in common?

Answer: They all love to see their names in the newspapers, especially in a favorable light.

Rank, position, or job classification are non-factors when it comes to the pleasure of seeing yourself quoted in the morning paper, the weekly magazine, or on the evening news on TV. The scenarios are virtually the same.

The wife or husband picks up the morning paper and excitedly flips through the pages looking for the article that quotes his or her spouse. A reporter had interviewed this loved one a few days earlier and the entire family has been tracking each edition for days, waiting for the pleasure of seeing that special name somewhere within. Not even the producer of a million-dollar Broadway play awaits the reviews of his production with greater eagerness.

When the article—or the TV interview—finally appears, all eyes light up. The family beams and pats the hero (or heroine) on the back. Neighbors call to say "I just saw it!" Fellow passengers at the train station congratulate the new celebrity. Colleagues drop by the office to rub elbows with the VIP who's just been in the media. Insurance agents add a new name to their "must call" list. He or she is—or *you are*—suddenly famous.

You've achieved that bit of fame, peer approval, and recognition simply by being in the news, by helping to make news. Few things can send us into as much rapture, regardless of race, creed, color, religious belief, occupation, or economic standing as being in the news. And few achievements face stiffer competition in the process.

Why, once you're in the media, does it seem so easy? How hard *is* it to get into the media?

How is it done? Can *you* do it? Enter public relations.

<u>CHAPTER THREE</u>

WHAT MAKES A GOOD PR PRACTITIONER?

A man steps into a phone booth and says the magic words, "Corporate Image." In a sudden flash of typewriter ribbon he becomes "PR Man"—a wide smile fixed on his face. His fingers flex in anticipation of countless handshakes, his mind forms strings of pleasant, glib words, his amino acids brace themselves for the four martinis he is expected to down during the traditional three-hour lunch.

He looks a bit like Tony Curtis in *Sweet Smell of Success*, with a touch of Jack Lemmon in *Days of Wine and Roses*.

Perspiration beads his brow as he anticipates the excitement and satisfaction of conning the world. No one knows precisely what he does—or how he does it—but he conveys glamour and intrigue.

Does this description fit a typical public relations executive? The movie industry seems to think so. But the typical public relations executive—if there is such a thing—looks more like your next-door neighbor than like Tony Curtis. In fact, if appearance is any indicator, he or she probably looks more like an accountant, lawyer, or doctor.

With the PR field growing rapidly, and with opportunities constantly opening up, I'm often asked what it takes to build a successful PR career. Here are the basics I look for:

A public relations executive

1. Must be an excellent writer capable of writing client reports, effective article themes to editors, news releases, captions, annual reports, feature stories, and the like. His or her writing must require little editing and supervision. He or she must also be proficient in all communications techniques used by public relations professionals, and able to translate the client's or company's products, services, and messages into readable English.

2. Must be able to do short- and long-range planning, conceive and execute a full public relations plan for each account, and adhere strictly to deadlines.

3. Must be innovative and imaginative, not bound by traditional journeymen ideas. Must be willing to keep an open mind to new ideas, to researching better ways.

4. Must be well-informed about a client's business and continue to keep abreast of all developments in business and government that have an effect on the client or company's business.

5. Must be able to function as a counselor as well as a communicator.

6. Must be results-oriented, whether the task is the placement of major stories about a client in important publications or the successful execution of a special event.

7. Must be a doer, a self-starter. Must know what follow-up means, and have a solid respect for timetables and deadlines.

8. Must be a thorough "pro," skilled in all the techniques used in the practice of public relations:

   a. Writing and distribution of news releases.

   b. Producing press kits.

   c. Running press conferences.

   d. Running special events, anniversaries, open houses.

   e. Knowing media and where to place publicity (what stories to take where and who's writing what; the editorial formats of magazines, weekly and monthly; the format of major syndicated columnists, wire services, daily newspapers, etc.).

   f. Must be familiar with feature writers, magazine contributors, and hot subjects currently being written about.

9. Must know how to *create* publicity by conceiving a meaningful idea and carrying it through to its conclusion so that maximum publicity is obtained. Must know how to create story ideas where none are evident and must know where to take them.

10. Must know how to establish and maintain acquaintanceship with key media people, since editorial contact is one of the primary publicity functions of the public relations professional. The question "which editors do you know?" is a valid one in our business. Experience shows that the more business relationships the individual has with various editors and producers, the greater the chances of acceptance of client and company story ideas. The public relations professional must know how to deal with the media and understand their need for quick and responsive answers.

11. Must be able to learn and grow as new situations and client needs arise. Must draw upon prior experience in the public relations field to move into new situations effortlessly and effectively.

12. Must be a good manager, capable of organizing and arranging his or her workload for maximum results. Must be capable of carrying many assignments at the same time, and be in control of each.

13. Finally, the public relations professional— whether he or she works for an agency, a corporation, a nonprofit institution, or in government—must not be a "yes" man/woman. Public relations has outgrown the caricature of second-class professionalism by producing individuals who speak their minds confidently to top management of major corporations and make valuable recommendations to these executives about the manner in which the company should conduct itself. So long as public relations professionals earn the respect and confidence of chief executive officers, public relations will grow as a profession and will contribute to the broad communications goals of companies and institutions across the United States.

Far too many chief executive officers of major corporations have distorted views of both public relations and the media. Some CEOs feel that their company's public relations officer should be able to place a positive story about his company in *The Wall Street Journal* simply by taking an editor to lunch. The same chief executive officers will urge their public relations managers to know as many business and financial writers as possible on a first-name basis so that they can get them to do "favors" for their company. While acquaintance with editors is very useful, reliance on the "buddy system" is an antiquated and obsolete notion. Media and public relations people do know each other on a first-name basis, of course, but this relationship can never guarantee placement of company stories in the media. What it can secure is a willing ear and access for the public relations professional, who can then state his case for consideration of a particular trend or development within a company.

Is there an ideal background for a successful career in public relations? No. It's not where you come from that's important, it's what you bring with you.

The fact is that almost without exception up until five or ten years ago, most public relations people got into it quite by accident. Members of the medical, legal, engineering, and teaching professions confront vigorous academic requirements, residency programs, and finally board and state certification. In other words, you need a license to practice those professions. You don't in public relations, advertising, and similar fields.

At one point, many of the people who entered PR came from journalism—once a notoriously underpaid field. Because the skills of public relations people and journalists are in many respects similar, journalism was a natural source of talent for the higher paying public relations field.

Thus, the field was made up very heavily of ex-reporters and editors. However, at one time the public relations field was so ill-defined that retired celebrities from various fields were tempted to launch new careers in public relations. It was embarrassing for public relations professionals when the former great heavyweight boxing champion of the world, Joe Louis, announced that he was starting a "public relations" firm to be called Joe Louis, Inc. This furthered the perception of some that public relations was no more than shaking hands, smiling a lot, and lending your name to whatever cause, product, or promotion came along with a buck. Joe Louis, of course, could no more practice public relations than I could win a boxing championship.

My path to, and through, the wonderful world of PR is typical of many. I got into public relations by accident. It wasn't planned, like planning to be a doctor or a lawyer. It just happened. Having been an English major at the City College of New York, it seemed natural to me that I would launch an illustrious career as an editor of a major publishing house. My fantasies told me that once entrenched in this career, I would discover the new William Faulkners and Ernest Hemingways of our time.

It didn't work out that way.

When I went to work for Prentice-Hall, they appointed me copy editor on such noteworthy projects as *Understanding Soil Agriculture* and *Irrigation for Fun and Profit*. Something told me that my literary ambitions were being sidetracked. After a year of unrequited love affairs with Holsteins and Guernseys, I decided to deal with humans once again. As I was pondering my next career move, fate intervened in the person of a textbook art director turned personnel supervisor.

A buddy of mine who spent his time drawing cows for the books I edited decided he'd had it with textbooks, too. Somehow he got himself interviewed for the job of personnel supervisor at Prentice-Hall. He was asked to write a job description and why his experience qualified him for it. Well, Hal couldn't write his way out of a paper bag and did the only thing he could think of under the circumstances. He asked me to write it for him.

Being politically wily, I realized that if I helped Hal get his job, he might, in turn, be able to help me find a more interesting job in the company. I immediately sat down and wrote an ode to personnel work that got Hal the job in a matter of days. Being joyously grateful, Hal kept his eyes and ears open for me. While I waited, I continued to edit books about maximizing the efficiency of dung for your crops and how to motivate your hens. I felt I was truly being punished for being brought up in a big city. Finally, after several more months of my intolerable servitude on the farm, Hal came through.

The president of Prentice-Hall had started a corporate public relations department about a year earlier, headed by a retired Air Force colonel who had had some public information experience. The good colonel, used to military ways, was attempting to build a huge department around him.

"But Hal," I asked my personnel director friend, "what the hell is public relations?"

"What difference does it make?" Hal replied. "Would you rather keep on editing dung books?"

Hal could be persuasive.

I was interviewed for the job of assistant to the director of public relations without the foggiest notion of what public relations was. That didn't seem to faze the colonel. His only concern was that I would be a "good soldier" and help him whip the department into an efficient, streamlined entity.

I was elated. Public relations. That glamorous field. The big time. I called my father right away.

"Guess what, dad. I got a promotion. I'm assistant to the director of public relations."

Long pause.

"That's very nice, son. But what's public relations?"

"Oh, dad, for heaven's sake. Public relations is . . . well, it's like . . . uh, you deal with the public a lot."

An even longer pause.

"That's very nice, son. As long as it makes you happy."

At that point I began poring over every book I could find on the subject of public relations and taking courses at New York University and The New School. After all, if I couldn't explain public relations to my father, maybe I ought to get to know a little about it.

I guess I caught on fairly well, because one year later, at the tender age of 25, I replaced the good colonel and became a very young public relations director of a fairly large American Stock Exchange company. And how it was done is one of those bittersweet stories out of what might be one of Prentice-Hall's own books on how to succeed in business while really trying.

The good colonel reported directly to John Powers, the president of the company, who could have been picked from central casting to be president of a company—any company. He was a tall, good-looking man with graying temples and horn-rimmed glasses. He had a combination father figure/strong executive image that made the secretaries quiver when he'd pass them in the corridors, flash his executive smile and say, "Good morning and how are you today?"

While I was learning public relations on the job and taking courses and reading books, I came to realize that good relations with a company's customers and markets were important and that public relations plays an important role in both. Prentice-Hall, one of the world's largest publishers of all types of books, was expanding its international operations at that time. The company had set up a subsidiary in Japan, and as John Powers spent more and more time there overseeing the company's operations, he fell in love with Japanese culture. This love affair soon began to translate into action as he sought to share his appreciation of Japanese culture with the employees of the company.

At Prentice-Hall's suburban world headquarters in Englewood Cliffs, New Jersey, Powers began installing pieces from his unique collection of Japanese paintings, sculpture, and ancient silk screens; they decorated every nook and cranny of the huge, sprawling two-level buildings.

One day an assortment of construction equipment turned up in the company's backyard. When it left, Mr. Powers had created a Japanese garden complete with gurgling stream, pagodas, the works. The only thing missing was an honest-to-God authentic half-moon-type Japanese bridge.

We were not to be disappointed.

John Powers had ordered a traditional "Benki Bashi" bridge, which was being sent in sections by ship to fit across the little stream in the garden. And now enter Art Stevens.

"Bob," I said to my boss, the colonel, "why don't we have a bridge-dedication ceremony?"

The idea was snapped up and I approached my new assignment with fervor. I met with the aide to the Japanese Consul-General in New York and explained my plan. He went for it and helped me get introductions to such Japanese-oriented organizations as the Nippon Club, the Asia Society, and the New York-Tokyo Sister City Affiliation. The idea began to take shape. After a series of meetings with Japanese dignitaries, American ambassador types and the like, a date was set. Prentice-Hall president Powers, Mayor Robert Wagner of New York, and His Excellency the Japanese Consul-General to the United States were to preside.

Then one day the hot line rang and I was summoned by the president. I didn't have time to be nervous. Everything was happening so quickly. THE PRESIDENT OF THE COMPANY WANTS TO SEE ME.

John Powers was reading an interoffice memo and seemed to be unaware of my presence. When I cleared my throat on cue, he looked up and put me through an up-and-down eye scan.

"Tell me, Art. If you were running the public relations department, just how would you do it?"

I gulped hard. It may have been the only time I came close to losing my cool. Fortunately, when things go right they really go all the way. Just the week before this surprise meeting, I had been reading a chapter from a textbook I'd been using for one of my classes on how to organize a public relations department. I confess I must credit the next 10 minutes of that meeting to the authors (Cutlip and Center) of that book. I recited virtually verbatim from that chapter, which was fresh in my mind. How else could I have answered his question? At that point I had been in public relations for less than a year. It was like going through the oral exam for a master's degree program.

Apparently I passed the test. When I had finished, there was another long pause. Then Powers looked me straight in the eye and said,: "Art, I'm making a major change in your department. I'm appointing you public relations director of Prentice-Hall. Your boss will be moved to another position within the company where we can better utilize his talents. From now on you will report directly to me. Congratulations!"

He held out his hand, flashed his famous executive smile, and buzzed his secretary to get on with a series of phone calls he had to make. It was a good thing I didn't have to linger. My knees were shaking and my legs were rubbery. I tried to make a suave exit from his office but stumbled over a Japanese pagoda. He never noticed. He was into the company's price/earnings ratio and the next quarter's profitability.

I called my father immediately.

"Dad, you'll never guess what just happened. I'm public relations director of Prentice-Hall."

(SAME DAMNED PAUSE) "That's nice, son. But what is public relations?"

I was ready for him this time. "Well, dad, according to *Public Relations News*, one of the respected newsletters of the public relations field, public relations is a management function that evaluates public attitudes, identifies the policies and procedures of an individual or an organization as they affect the public interest, and executes a program of action to earn public understanding and acceptance. Implicit in this definition is the function of the professional public relations expert, which is threefold: to ascertain and evaluate public opinion, to counsel management on ways of dealing with public opinion as it exists, and to use communications to influence public opinion."

You guessed it—long pause. Then, "Uh, yes, I see. As long as you're happy."

That's how my career took off. Today there are more formal ways to prepare for the field (although I doubt that they are as much fun). Many colleges and universities offer majors in public relations; one of the most noteworthy programs is at Boston University. All facets of public relations are taught and graduates of these schools are almost assured of entry-level positions in public relations.

Lewis Carter, a partner in the Boston public relations firm Agnew, Carter, McCarthy, Inc., notes that job opportunities for PR majors vary significantly by region.

"In the Boston market, for example, there are many more entry-level people looking for jobs in the public relations field than there are jobs available. One reason for this is that many young people who go to college in Boston stay here to live. And there may be more colleges in the Boston area offering public relations courses than anywhere in the country."

Because his firm can be more selective in choosing entry-level job candidates than firms in other parts of the country, Carter's primary criterion for hiring is attitude.

"We're looking for young people who can sell themselves. If they can sell themselves to us, they can subsequently sell their work to our clients."

Whatever the background, the skills needed for success in PR are essentially the same—the ability to communicate well, verbally and in writing, and the exercise of sound judgment and common sense.

We look for evidence of these skills in a writing test our firm asks all candidates to take. The intent of the writing test is to identify both writing skills and sound judgment. If a candidate passes this test with flying colors, we grab that person.

Account Executive Test

Please read the following carefully and follow the instructions afterward. You will have one hour to carry out the assignment.

Gold is the ideal substance to use in dental work. Other materials are rated as to how closely they approach the performance of gold. The overwhelming consensus among dentists is that gold is easier to work with; it is completely inert and there is virtually no history of human allergy; it reacts to wear and temperature in a manner similar to teeth; and there are documented studies covering many years of experience with gold that do not exist for substitutes.

However, the use of gold in dental work has been declining rapidly because of the perception that gold is expensive and because the dentist thinks he will make less profit by using gold than nonprecious metals.

The consumer, in turn, seldom suggests what material should be used by the dentists. The patient listens as the dentist explains what should be done to correct his or her problem. When the subject of cost arises, however, the consumer is no longer passive.

The patient wants the work done, and done not only correctly, but inexpensively. The dentist is quite apt to state that nothing is as good as gold, but that the cost of the work can be reduced and a serviceable product obtained by using a substitute material.

In fact, perceptions aside, the cost of gold to the dentist is barely more than the cost of other materials because he uses a very small amount per dental restoration unit.

And yet the long-term benefits of gold in dental work are considerable.

Your Assignment

You have been hired to carry out a program to promote the use of gold in dentistry by the association of dental gold manufacturers.

1. Write a one-page news release (feature) making a case for the use of gold in dentistry. We are aware that you are not in possession of all the pertinent facts and information. However, we have no objection to your fabricating spokespeople, facts, and quotes in drafting this release. We are looking for concise, journalistic style; good lead; proper use of quotes; and persuasive prose.

2. Based on the information presented to you, write what you feel is an effective pitch letter to either one target publication or broadcast outlet or a series of them. In this letter, focus on an article idea or program segment you believe will be of

interest to an editor/producer and present the idea
in the best way you can. Explain your choice of
media.

3. Finally, think of how you would approach
   organizing and servicing this account. What kinds
   of events, projects, themes, etc. List these briefly
   and be prepared to discuss them with us.

Thank you very much for your cooperation.

Once PR was male-dominated. Today, however, public relations offers striking opportunities to women. The former president of the Public Relations Society of America is a woman;
50 percent of the executive positions in PRSA are held by women
and 40 percent of its current members are women. Although
PR was one of the first professions to open its doors to women
for high executive positions, until fairly recently these women
executives handled accounts considered their "specialty"—
fashion, food, household wares, baby products. Now, however, more and more women are emerging as public relations
executives in companies once dominated by men—insurance,
oil, broadcasting, finance, and utilities.

A growing number of women also are starting their own
public relations firms. A PR business can be launched with a
relatively small outlay of capital. What is required is a capacity
for hard work. My partner, Amelia Lobsenz, started out as a
freelance magazine writer and opened her own PR agency
before merging with mine. From the beginning her skills as a
magazine writer proved highly valuable for public relations
work; she was particularly successful in attracting clients interested in publicity in magazines.

Amelia's advice for women who wish to go into public relations: Select an area for which you have special skills; take
courses in public relations; study to remain constantly abreast
of the latest developments in your profession.

A number of women who have established highly successful
PR firms came from the book publishing industry, where they

gained experience and developed media contacts while arranging TV appearances and newspaper interviews for authors. Other women have set up public relations businesses in their own homes, incorporating their PR activities into their schedules as housewives and mothers. They operate with small overhead expenses and the advantage of working their own hours.

The inroads that women have made into the PR field have been documented by Edward Gottlieb, who once headed one of the fastest-growing PR agencies in the business. The agency was sold to Hill & Knowlton. Ed now serves as a consultant. He estimates that women now constitute more than 50 percent of the staffs at PR agencies and corporations. Charlotte Klein, the president of the New York chapter of the Public Relations Society of America in 1984, was employed by Gottlieb when he was running his own agency. He had given her responsibility for handling the toy industry. "Since the customers of toys are children, this seemed a natural assignment for a woman," Ed explains. She did such a splendid job that Ed decided to take what at that time was a novel and risky step— give her a shot at a corporate account that had been handled traditionally only by men—Chesebrough Ponds. "It took six months to get the Chesebrough brass to accept the idea of a woman managing its account but she won their confidence and later, as noted, became president of the New York chapter of PRSA."

One of my top executives is Mari Gold, who has been highly successful in staffing her team with women. "A good public relations practitioner has a lot in common with a really effective household manager," Mari points out. "She has to be skillful in juggling a million details. She must keep a lot of people happy simultaneously." Mari looks for a bright, outgoing personality in her staffers. A job-seeker need not be a highly skilled writer. Being a good writer is certainly important but being a good communicator on the phone and in person is much more so. "In pursuing an account," observes Ms. Gold, "you have to be tenacious in a very nice way. You can't overdo it to the point of being rude but you have to hang in there. If a woman is too shy, she shouldn't take up public relations. I want someone who knows how to persuade people, whether or not she is an excellent writer. You can be trained to write."

Persuasiveness, style, and charm are the three ingredients Mari looks for. "I walk around the office and overhear what my people are saying to their clients. The really good ones are friendly without being overbearing and gracious without being obsequious. They make the story they have to tell very persuasive, and let me tell you, since they are telling that same story for the fourth or the twenty-fourth time, they'd better be tenacious or they are in the wrong business."

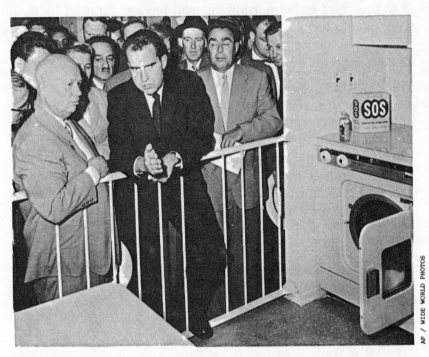

When he helped steer Vice President Richard Nixon and Soviet Premier Nikita Khrushchev into a typical American kitchen during an international trade fair in Moscow, William Safire was able to engineer the famous "kitchen debate." The reputation Nixon gained for being able to talk back to the Russians sent his political star soaring.

CHAPTER FOUR

SUCCESS DOES SMELL SWEET

My agency has done well. It is often said that success makes you bored and jaded. Not me. There is intense satisfaction, every minute of the day, in executing strategies that bring a client to favorable public attention. And there is great satisfaction when my firm's ability and reputation are acknowledged in the most meaningful of all ways—the winning of new accounts.

One of the great joys of being in the public relations agency field is the adventure of new business pursuits. My firm is by no means the largest public relations firm in the country, but we are known for our enthusiasm, perseverance, dedication, and lively pursuit of new business. Since new business is the lifeblood of any agency, it must be pursued vigorously and decisively.

A case in point. We received what was obviously a form letter from a Pennsylvania-based conglomerate inviting us to submit a proposal for their account. I asked one of my executives to immediately telephone the signer of the letter to arrange for a meeting. Being well-versed in our aggressive pursuit of new business, my executive telephoned the company official, but was not able to reach him. He left a message.

Knowing that I do not accept as an excuse the fact that one of my people left a message for someone, my executive continued to call the company official repeatedly, leaving a string of messages. After at least six phone calls went unanswered, the company official finally called back. He apologized for not returning calls earlier and promptly set a date for a meeting. My executive and another member of our team drove to Pennsylvania and met with the company official and several of his colleagues. Immediately upon their return, they burst into my office beaming. They explained the unanswered calls. The company official had set out to determine which public relations firms should wind up on the so-called short list. A short list is generally a list of three finalists from among a much greater number that initially participated in the selection process.

To measure the extent of interest on the part of the public relations firms he had written to, he decided not to answer any initial calls that came to him to see which of the public relations agencies were sufficiently interested in his account to continue to try to reach him. Of the 15 companies he had written to originally, four didn't respond at all, four dispatched written proposals without having met with the prospect, four put in an initial telephone call and when the call was not returned didn't bother to continue their efforts, and three continued to call—despite not having their initial calls returned—to set up meetings.

The three firms who persisted in attempting to set up a fact-finding meeting became the finalists. We were one of them and we subsequently got the account.

The moral is that if you want new business, go for it. Do not concern yourself with calls that are not returned. Continue to call. No one was ever offended that I repeatedly put in phone calls to them when I was attempting to reach them for new business. Quite the contrary. My perseverance and my genuine interest always paid off.

Persistence does indeed pay huge dividends. Just as in the

boy-girl courting game, when people feel you want them badly enough they become more responsive and receptive.

Although I am an agency president who has achieved some degree of success in the agency field, I never allow myself to forget the importance of humility. No matter who I call on the telephone, I place all my own calls. I have never allowed my secretary to dial a number for me. I am never too proud to tell a new business prospect how much I want his account. I will never walk into a new business situation unprepared or insufficiently briefed.

I like to remind my colleagues about Pete Rose, the durable professional baseball player. Rose became known as "Charlie Hustle" because he always went after every ball in the field and ran out every ball he hit as hard as he could. He played to win, and obviously won often. If we play to win, we have to hustle also. There's a lot of competition out there that would love for us to be complacent. You don't succeed in this business by being complacent. When a client senses that you will literally break your back to do the best possible job for him, it is to his advantage to choose you.

That's the way I have always conducted my professional life and it is the rallying cry I pass on to all who work with and for me.

In the public relations agency field, it is axiomatic that a firm is successful if it is able to pull in three accounts out of every ten it is considered for. I don't believe in that at all. I believe strongly that my firm is justified in feeling that it should be chosen for ten out of ten. I am not a good loser. I will not spend the day dwelling on accounts we have not won, but nobody should be near me when the call comes in from a new business prospect that we were not chosen. I am not happy when such calls come in, but ultimately I feel that the loss is the prospect's and not ours. In my heart I always feel that he has done his company a disservice by not choosing my firm.

The selection process for choosing a PR firm is often long and tortuous. Many factors enter into the decision, not the least of which are style, chemistry, and personality. I believe that ultimately a client prospect, when weighing the final decision, asks himself which of the candidate firms his company can work with most harmoniously.

Once the decision is made the new business prospect has the sad duty to inform the runners-up and the pleasant duty to inform the winner. Whenever we are told we have won an account, the phone calls are joyous and can sometimes bring tears. I personally react very strongly when a call comes in to inform me that my agency has been selected, practically turning somersaults in my office and erupting with screams of joy. There is nothing as invigorating or stimulating to the personnel of a public relations firm than to be told it's a winner. Winning a new account builds esprit de corps, morale, and motivation. Employees feel they're part of a winning team and that their firm is on the move. I can only liken it to rooting for a winning team in sports.

I have been the recipient of some very pleasant telephone calls announcing my firm as the winner in a public relations agency selection process. On two separate occasions, I was called on Christmas Eve with the good news. One occasion involved the New York State Lottery.

My firm has been working with the New York State Lottery for more than eight years. Every two years we must go through another competitive selection process because, as a state agency, the lottery is obliged to make certain that its various services are open to periodic competitive bidding during one of these renewal processes. I was sitting home with my family one Christmas Eve, about to celebrate the holiday, when the phone rang. My wife took the call and told me that it was John Quinn, the director of the New York State Lottery. It didn't take great logic on my part to figure out that John Quinn was not calling me on Christmas Eve to tell me that my firm had lost the account. And for the first time in my professional life, I decided to turn the situation around during one of these get-the-word phone calls. Before Quinn had a chance to tell me anything, I said to him, "John, you're too good to be true. I know what you're about to say and I want you to know that we accept, are honored, and are deeply grateful that you would take the time on Christmas Eve to call to tell me that we have won the account."

There was a long awkward pause on the phone and I began to wonder if my logic had indeed been correct. Not to be discouraged.

"You tricky son of a gun," laughed Quinn. "You stole my thunder. But of course you had to realize I wasn't calling you on Christmas Eve just to wish you a happy holiday. Congratulations to you and your fine team. It's my pleasure to be able to present this Christmas present to you in this way."

On yet another Christmas Eve I received a long distance call from Winston Burrell, the Minister of Tourism of Trinidad/ Tobago. Here again, my firm had been among the top ten and we had no idea if we were even going to make the final three. But this was also to be a joyous Christmas because he called to say that we had stood out from the crowd quite convincingly and it was his pleasure to give us this Christmas present at this time. It happened that he called minutes before our annual office Christmas party and I was able to surprise the staff by telling them we were no longer a long shot in the selection process for the Trinidad/Tobago account—but that we had actually won it. Joy to the world!

Winning new business is not an exact science. Once we were competing against four other firms for a major Midwest food account. In preparing for our presentation we shot the works— elaborate flip charts, a dramatic slide presentation—a real dog and pony show.

With two colleagues I entered the conference room to make the presentation. More than a dozen people sat around the table; a large group for this sort of occasion. But we were ready. We launched into our show, dimmed the lights, began to put on our slides. We were feeling good, really rolling. Then, from the darkness, came a sound that curdled our blood— a faint snore. As the slide show proceeded the snoring got louder, *louder*, LOUDER! The lights went up to reveal, at the head of the table, the president—fast asleep.

What to do? We were crushed. The president's colleagues were in a quandary. It would be embarrassing to nudge him. One of his henchmen solved the problem by bellowing, "Okay! Let's take a ten-minute coffee break!" The president came to with a start. His confusion was covered by the general bustle. He didn't look at us, we didn't look at him.

After the break we went through the rest of our presentation, packed up, got on the plane. We were a glum group. We had blown it in the worst possible way, by putting the prospect to sleep.

Two days later we got a call. It was the president of the food company himself: "I want to congratulate you on a wonderful presentation—*particularly* the slide show. It was dramatic and entertaining. You've got the account."

Afterward we toyed with the idea that the key to success was inducing sleep in the prospect. We decided not to try it— at least not consciously.

Well-established PR firms are approached by prospective clients whose products and services range from totally conventional to off-the-wall. An example of the latter: the gentleman who came to us with the news that he had acquired, from NASA, real estate rights on the moon. His plan was to appeal to persons who wanted to be buried on the moon. These customers would contract with our prospective client to be sent by rocket (after they had died, of course) to the great cemetery in the sky. The gentleman wanted a public relations program to acquaint everyone with this extraordinary opportunity.

Much as I dislike dampening anyone's dream, I asked him to come back in 50 years. Off-the-wall projects are not unusual in this field, but this one was literally out-of-this-world.

Despite the fact that my firm is often on a list of five to ten public relations firms considered by new business prospects, I personally prefer to pursue new business without competition. In other words, I simply would like a new business prospect to call me and say, "I've heard about your firm, I like its style, and we have chosen you to be our public relations firm." This doesn't happen very often, but often enough to make up for any account we don't get through the highly competitive, multiple agency selection process. It's like a gift from heaven. There's no question that the feeling is quite different from being chosen a winner from a field of highly competent competitors. It's like the New York Yankees not having to play out their full baseball schedule and being invited to the World Series on the basis of their past performance. I'll take it anytime, but I must admit, I love that sweet smell of success that comes with winning in a competitive heat.

CHAPTER FIVE

TEX MCCRARY AND MODERN PUBLIC RELATIONS

One of the joys of public relations is people. I am constantly meeting and working with fascinating people: PR practitioners, clients, journalists, and, indeed, the vast range of humanity. PR is truly a people-oriented business.

Those from whom we learn the basics of our work make an indelible impression on our lives. I have been lucky in knowing, and learning from, masters.

"Tex" McCrary, for instance, has done as much as anyone to shape the profession. He started in the "Front Page" era of tabloid journalism as a reporter (subsequently chief editorial writer) for the New York *Daily Mirror*. After earning his spurs in the tough, competitive world of 1930's journalism, he turned his talents to public relations.

At that time PR was still evolving from the days of the press agent. Its most important pioneer in the United States was Edward L. Bernays. Bernays, the nephew of Sigmund Freud, was a press agent for Enrico Caruso. When the great tenor was arrested for pinching a woman (how times have changed!), it appeared that his career might be over, golden voice or not. Bernays was highly instrumental in enabling Caruso to weather the storm and regain public affection. Once, during the imbroglio, Bernays was called upon to testify in court. Asked his occupation, he did not reply "press agent." Instead he proclaimed, "*I am a counsel on public relations.*" The newspapers picked it up. Bernays had given a name to the profession. Even more, he had given it scope and direction. "Counsel on public relations" obviously encompassed far more than mere press agentry.

Public relations men of that era tended to be flamboyant individuals who retained the flair of the fabled press agents. One of the great ones was Ivy Lee.

Lee's role in the history of public relations began early in the century, thanks to Arthur Brisbane, one of the founding fathers of mass journalism. Brisbane, a close friend of William Randolph Hearst and editorial director of the Hearst chain of newspapers, was given the assignment of shoring up the sagging reputation of oil tycoon John D. Rockefeller, who had infuriated the public with his ruthless business dealings. (In those days the line between journalism and PR was blurred or nonexistent, particularly with Brisbane.) Tired of continually "saving Rockefeller from the lynch mob" by writing editorials apologizing for his behavior, Brisbane had a hunch. He had noticed during a violent strike in the coal mines in 1906 that a young writer on the payroll of the mine operators had successfully placed articles in the newspapers presenting the case of the owners so persuasively that the strike was broken. Brisbane induced Rockefeller to hire this young man—Ivy Lee— to help him improve his image with the American public.

Ivy Lee persuaded Rockefeller that the best way to erase his reputation of being a capitalist "Scrooge" would be to hand out dimes to whomever he met in the streets. Lee got the old curmudgeon to walk down the main streets of America, dipping into his pocket and handing out dimes while the cameras clicked. This picturesque gesture, repeated over and over again, completely reversed Rockefeller's unfavorable image; Americans came to regard the once-reviled capitalist as a benevolent old man. The job that Ivy Lee did laid the foundations of the modern public relations profession. Until Lee's inspired maneuver, public relations had confined itself to stunts generated by press agents to promote circus and carnival shows. Ivy Lee broadened the application of PR as a means of changing the image of individuals and businesses in every walk of life.

Which brings us back to Tex McCrary. McCrary married Arthur Brisbane's daughter. His close and enduring relationship with Brisbane helped him to marshal his intelligence and flair to become a virtuoso of PR.

McCrary has always been a thorough professional. This does not mean he misses the opportunity for an impressive stunt in a good cause. McCrary has told me how his father-in-law, Brisbane, while carrying on officially as a journalist, privately waved the magic wand of public relations for the benefit of clients of his newspapers. One was Walter Chrysler, the founder of the Chrysler Auto Company. At one point the Chrysler people ran an advertising slogan, "If there is a better car to build, Chrysler will build it." And since Walter Chrysler was a major advertiser in his newspapers, Brisbane advised him on how to promote his business. He suggested that the slogan should be run with a picture of Walter Chrysler addressing the American public. Brisbane spent hours coaching Chrysler on what kind of picture to take. He had Chrysler pose shouting out his slogan; he had him singing songs; he tried other devices to get the proper exalted expression on Chrysler's face. Finally, to obtain the most effective picture, Brisbane resorted to subterfuge. He took the head of Walter Chrysler singing and put it on the body of Billy Sunday, the popular evangelist preacher, whose arms were extended in a call for converts to Christ.

McCrary's progress in his new profession was spectacular. When the United States entered World War II he was able to put his skills to work for the country. He became public relations officer of the Allied Air Force operating in the Mediterranean. A fanatical supporter of air power, he organized a flying air exhibition for the AAF. And with a group of Air Force newspaper correspondents, he entered Nagasaki and Hiroshima shortly after the atomic bombs fell. He was one of the first American eyewitnesses to observe the results of the holocaust. Doffing his uniform at the end of the war, he moved into the infant field of television, appreciating that it was destined to become a dominating influence in our civilization. He produced, along with his wife, Jinx Falkenberg, a beautiful model, and film and tennis star, several pioneer news television shows.

Tex used the new art form of television to perfection. He opened one show with a close-up of two scorpions fighting inside an empty wine flask. After a few seconds, during which the scorpions battled one another to death, a voice came on saying that this was the current state of the world; America and the Soviet Union were playing the roles of scorpions locked in a death struggle.

After a dissolve, a guest appeared. He was U. Baughman, head of the U.S. Secret Service. The camera focused on a metal object Mr. Baughman held in his hand. This, he explained, had been passed from each head of the Secret Service to his successor during the last 70 years. It guaranteed that the Secret Service would never forget its number one mission in a world even then rampant with terrorism. What was this metal object, McCrary asked his guest? "It's the bullet that killed Abraham Lincoln."

Tex is fond of observing, "The PR practitioner doesn't go along with the action; he *makes it happen.*" Every year Tex spends Christmas in a different part of the world. And on each occasion he devises a public relations coup. In 1948 he spent Christmas in Berlin with the American Air Force. This was during an historic confrontation with the Russians. The Soviets had blockaded Berlin, cutting it off from ground communications with the West. The American Air Force, in defiance, was flying food and supplies into the blockaded city in a continual shuttle operation going on night and day. It was a critical period and everything hinged upon sustaining the morale of the American flyers engaged in the Berlin airlift. Tex contacted President Truman, suggesting that he send over his vice president to read a message of Christmas greetings to the troops. Then McCrary called up comedian Bob Hope from Berlin, asking him to fly in to entertain the troops. Hope retorted, "Me leave home on Christmas Day? No way! Delores, my wife, would divorce me. If you don't believe me, here's Delores." Hope put her on the phone and she reiterated "No way!"

No public relations expert worth his salt is easily daunted by any roadblock thrown up to thwart him. Tex phoned Ellen Berlin, wife of the famous songwriter, who was an old friend. "Ellen, how would you like to get Irving back into his World War I uniform? I want him to enter Berlin with the vice president of the United States and sing 'White Christmas' and 'God Bless America' on the stage of the Berlin Opera House where no Jew has been able to perform since the rise of Hitler!" There was a moment of silence, "Irving's packing his trunk!" Ellen exploded. Tex called Bob Hope back and when the comedian heard that Irving Berlin was going to Berlin he quickly changed his mind and hopped a plane. Thus began Hope's yearly routine of entertaining American troops all over the world on Christmas.

Christmas in West Germany that year was a thunderous success. The morale of the U.S. Air Force was tremendously buoyed. The blockade was broken and the Russians were forced to restore free access to Berlin to the Allies. Public relations is clearly more than selling a personality or a product when it can help win a critical battle in a war for freedom.

McCrary has fine-tuned his craft for the benefit of U.S. presidents. He has advised Reagan, Nixon, and Eisenhower on how to present themselves with the maximum effectiveness before the American public. For instance, he noticed in 1980, when Reagan was running for the presidency, that he was having trouble hearing reporters' questions. Reagan told him that the hearing in his right ear had been shattered years previously during the making of a movie when another actor had shot off a revolver near him. Tex immediately launched a private, man-to-man campaign to persuade Reagan to forgo his vanity and start wearing a hearing aid. He not only spoke to the president himself, but to his chief advisors, warning them that Reagan's hearing disability was adversely affecting his image as a communicator. It took three years of effort on the part of McCrary and other presidential counselors, but finally the president took the advice and adopted a hearing aid. His move pleased the medical community when it encouraged many hearing-impaired persons, who had until then been reluctant to wear hearing aids, to take the same step. Tex had previously dealt with another celebrity on the same matter, financier Bernard Baruch, who finally yielded to McCrary's persuasion and accepted a hearing device.

Tex is fond of quoting an observation once made by Fred Allen, the old-time comedian. "My best ad libs are the ones I've rehearsed the most." It's been the same way with Tex's most "inspirational" PR moves. Everyone says that John F. Kennedy was the first president to brilliantly exploit television as a public relations tool. But according to McCrary, it was Eisenhower who was the first to make use of television to this end. McCrary played a crucial role in helping to make Eisenhower President of the United States. In June 1951, when Eisenhower was still Supreme Commander of NATO Forces in Europe, McCrary flew over with Bernard Baruch to talk Eisenhower into running for the presidency on the Republican ticket. Tex felt that Ike, because of his popularity, would be a "natural" to defeat the Democrats who had had a strangle hold on the White House since the days of Franklin D. Roosevelt. Ike had previously announced to the press that he did not wish to enter politics. He had gone back in uniform to unify the West European Allies against the threat of the Communists, he observed, and wanted nothing to do with politicians.

However, he could not refuse to see an old friend like Barney Baruch. So Baruch and McCrary were welcomed by Ike at his headquarters at SHAPE.

Ike was putting a golf ball into a highball glass on his rug, taking one practice shot after another. It was his way of telling his visitors, "Look, I'm not going to get serious, chaps." They all sat down, Ike keeping his putter on his lap, indicating "let's not talk too long because I've got to get back to my golf." After the opening pleasantries, Mr. Baruch said abruptly, "General, one year from today in Chicago I predict you will be nominated on the Republican ticket for the presidency of the United States. Tex here will explain all the details to you." Ike blinked, swallowed hard, put his putter down and listened seriously to his visitors' plans.

McCrary organized a midnight rally for Eisenhower in Madison Square Garden just before the New Hampshire primaries. Bill Safire, who worked for Tex at the time, assisted him in the planning and organization of the event. It was Safire's first major experience in the use of public relations in political campaigning. The Garden was packed to the rafters even though the rally took place at midnight in the middle of a severe blizzard. It was the uproarious welcome that he received at the Garden, Ike said later, that helped persuade him to run for the presidency.

During the campaign McCrary was Eisenhower's public relations consultant. He told Ike, "Don't ever forget that television is as personal as a telephone conversation. Do what you did so eloquently with the troops. Talk to the cameraman personally. Speak to him as you would speak to one of your sergeants on the battlefield when you asked him if he had received mail from home."

Tex taught Eisenhower the secret of projecting charm on the podium. A candidate should seem to be speaking on a one-to-one basis with every member of his audience. He told Eisenhower to read the scripts of Churchill's great speeches. He would find that Churchill had written down, in the margin, the specific names of people seated in the audience he was addressing so that when he reached a certain paragraph he could look directly at that person and speak to him personally. Franklin Roosevelt would do the same whenever he got to a certain paragraph because Robert E. Sherwood, who prepared his speeches, was an expert playwright who always kept the audience in mind.

Presidential politics, has, of course, been a major theater for public relations. Ronald Reagan is generally considered to be the president with the greatest mastery of television for political purposes. The seemingly effortless charm and homespun persuasiveness that Reagan projects when he appears on television are actually the result of meticulous calculations. It is a scrupulously learned "effortlessness."

McCrary also put his talents to work for Reagan. During the latter's 1981 run for the White House, McCrary realized that the problem was more than hiring brilliant writers to draft effective speeches for Reagan. After analyzing him for several months on the campaign trail, McCrary told Reagan that in his opinion he had gotten through to the American people only once in a really effective way. That was during his acceptance speech for the Republican nomination. At the end of a bunch of cliches, McCrary reminded Reagan, "You lowered your head and said, 'will you join me in a moment of silent prayer for America, the last best hope of the world?' and you lowered your head and you got through to everybody. I could feel it at the back of my head. I could feel it in my nose and up my spine."

What McCrary had suddenly grasped was that Reagan had the rare ability to make down-home corniness sincere. McCrary advised the president to use this asset to the hilt.

The first occasion on which the new president could put this advice to work was at a session with a group of soldiers who had won the Medal of Honor. They were attending a dinner and the president was scheduled to address them. McCrary told Reagan, he reported to me afterward, that this was going to be one of the most significant audiences anybody ever had since George Washington said farewell to his troops in Manhattan and Lincoln delivered his Gettysburg Address. "You've got Medal of Honor men out there in the audience," he reminded the president, adding that it was a Medal of

Honor man who had induced Ike Eisenhower to finally take the plunge and run for the presidency. "I told him that this same Medal of Honor man was sitting out there in the audience: that the president should speak directly to him." A surprise had been arranged in staging this ceremony—one that Reagan had not been apprised of. At the end of the speech the Medal of Honor veteran McCrary spoke about came up to the podium and presented the president with a Patriot's Award. When Reagan, completely unaware of what was coming, was handed the gold medal, he took it, held it and said, "It's so easy to love America, I do not know why I should get a medal for it." And then he spontaneously added a phrase that made headlines all over the nation—words that in fact became the most widely quoted of his presidency, "America is standing tall again."

Sums up McCrary, "That, of course, is Ronald Reagan, pure Ronald Reagan." The president had finally succeeded in releasing the true man; allowing himself to come through simply, directly, and sincerely to the American people. This is why today he is hailed as the Great Communicator.

What applies to presidents also applies to everybody else. The major challenge confronting each one of us is how to become a more expert and articulate communicator. This is the key to success and power.

Tex has always been an avid believer in the power of words. His father-in-law, Arthur Brisbane, advised him when he was starting out in his own career, "Learn to write—to reach the people who move their lips when they read and follow a line with their finger. When you learn that technique, you will know how to talk to the Presidents of the United States."

CHAPTER SIX

BILL SAFIRE: A GEM OF A PR MAN

Today William Safire, truly a man to learn from, plays two important roles in American political and cultural life. He is the respected and influential political columnist of *The New York Times*, whose judgments and predictions are read and quoted by both political insiders and the public at large. And he has assumed the mantle of the late H. L. Mencken as one of the supreme arbiters of popular usage of the English language.

Bill Safire's deep insight into human motivations and great skill with words, combined with his love for the language, make him eminent in his new fields. In his former vocations they made him a master public relations man and presidential adviser. He has made a momentous difference in my life.

In 1966, after seven fruitful, rewarding years at Prentice-Hall, I made the decision to move on. I had a comfortable position as the public relations director of one of the biggest firms in the publishing business. But publishing is a small, specialized field and there was a vast, tempting PR world beyond, brimming with exciting new challenges. I was eager to explore the field of general public relations, to work in an agency that handled a wide variety of clients instead of just one. I felt I needed this experience to round out my education as a PR man.

At this juncture a friend phoned me and told me that William Safire was looking for an account executive for his public relations firm. "Do you know of anybody who might be interested in the job?" "How about me?" I shot back. My friend was taken by surprise. He had been unaware of my restlessness.

Safire, who had started out working for Tex McCrary and subsequently founded his own agency, quickly displayed his brilliance by devising highly successful public relations campaigns for Mayor John Lindsay, Senator Jacob Javits, and Governor Nelson Rockefeller. Safire's most notable coup was on behalf of Richard Nixon when the latter was Vice-President, engineering the historic "kitchen debate" between Nixon and Soviet Premier Khrushchev which took place in 1959 during an American National Exhibition in Moscow. Safire was at that time doing PR for an American kitchenware manufacturer who was displaying equipment at the U.S. trade exhibition in Moscow. Vice-President Nixon was visiting Russia and, as part of the ceremonies, was scheduled to take Khrushchev for a walk through the U.S. exhibition to show him products illustrating America's style of life.

Bill Safire was present in Sokolniki Park as Nixon and Khrushchev, accompanied by their aides, walked from one exhibit to another. By a stroke of luck the two leaders drifted toward an area showing a "typical American home" where Safire's client was displaying its kitchenwares. The leaders were halted for a few moments by a surging crowd. As they stood hesitantly, Safire, from his position in front of his client's stove, called out in an authoritative tone, "Right this way— right this way!" Nixon and Khrushchev, thinking they were being directed by a secret service agent, walked up to the stove and for a few seconds paused in front of it, engaging in animated conversation as they waited for a path to be cleared through the mob. It was a fantastic moment to take a picture of Nixon arguing with Khrushchev, pointing as he did so to the chromium-plated stove as a symbol of America's high standard of living. A photographer for the Associated Press, attempting to take a picture of Khrushchev and Nixon, was shoved back into the crowd. He noticed that Safire was standing just a few feet from the two men. Holding his camera above his head, he lobbed it like a basketball over the heads of the people in front of him to Safire, who caught it, focused on Khrushchev and Nixon and snapped the most important picture of his life. He captioned it "Kitchen Conference" and it made the front pages all over the world. Nixon's gesture, pointing his finger into Khrushchev's face to prove that he was not afraid to talk back to the Russian premier, fired the imagination of millions. Overnight the American Vice-President was transformed from a figure known only to his countrymen into a celebrity around the globe—the man who told the Russians off.

Nixon was deeply impressed when he learned how Bill Safire had taken this epochal photograph. Bill became his close friend and advisor, at his side through the good and the bad times. He played a major role in masterminding the public relations campaign and much of the political strategy that resurrected Nixon's career and catapulted him into the White House. As president-elect, Nixon asked Safire to join him to be Special Assistant to the President and chief speech writer. While serving in the White House, Safire wrote a number of speeches for both the president and Vice-President Agnew, introducing Agnew's celebrated alliterative phrase-making, which became widely quoted in the press ("nattering nabobs of negativism," for one).

But I am getting ahead of my story. At the time I walked into Bill Safire's office and applied for a job, although he was only in his mid-thirties, Bill had already achieved considerable renown.

He occupied offices in the Seagram Building in midtown Manhattan. His own quarters took up half the total space. It was a posh setting festooned with trophies from his career—

framed letters from Nixon on the wall, photographs of other widely known politicos he had helped guide to victory.

Safire looked up and came directly to the point, "So you're PR director of Prentice-Hall. What do you know about public relations?" I went through the litany of activities I had been involved with. Bill interrupted me; "here's the deal." He offered me a very modest salary. "That's as high as I'll go. Take it or leave it." I took it.

Working for Safire proved to be quite a learning experience. He bristled with idiosyncracies. Whenever he plunged deep into thought, he'd begin to hum a melody off key. You could always tell when Bill was wrestling with a problem by this out-of-tune humming. I would walk down the street with him, engaged in conversation, and all of a sudden he would lapse into silence and then begin humming his unrecognizable tune. He would do the same in the middle of a business conference.

Safire exulted in problem-solving, which he did brilliantly. He had an uncanny knack of progressing through a series of logical steps that would unerringly guide his clients to the correct solution. This genius for getting to the heart of a complex problem and coming up with the right answer was demonstrated to me time and again. I would do research on a client's problem and walk into Bill's office with an armful of statistics announcing, "here are the issues as I see them." Safire would quickly leaf through my papers, spring up from his desk, and walk back and forth for five minutes humming his mysterious melody while I sat watching him, knowing that the wheels were furiously turning in his brain. Then he'd suddenly stop. "Okay, here is the campaign we'll run." And he'd proceed to map out, step by step, in the most intricate fashion, the campaign that we were to follow. It reminded me of a scene in the office of a Hollywood movie producer: as the studio brain trust struggles to come up with a plot for a movie, the script writer suddenly jumps up and says, "This is it," then nonchalantly improvises a scenario in precise detail from start to finish.

Bill Safire has long had a special passion for America's political scene. He had gotten his feet wet working with the Eisenhower forces in their successful attempt to wrest the presidential nomination from Senator Robert Taft at the 1952 Republican convention. His work for Eisenhower resulted in calls by Mayor Lindsay and Senator Javits to handle public relations during their campaigns for office.

Shortly after I joined Safire I became involved in a local political campaign that was to have a crucial impact on the fortunes of Nixon, insuring his victory in the presidential race of 1968. The campaign was held in Essex County, New Jersey, in 1967 and our clients were a slate of reform Republican candidates. New Jersey was a bellwether state, critical to Republican presidential chances the following year. Safire had been hired to conduct a campaign for 22 of these reform Republican candidates running for a variety of local offices, including the State Assembly, the Senate, the Board of Freeholders, and Office of Sheriff. Essex County had been in the hands of the Democrats for 20 years. Long out of office and starved for success, the Jersey Republicans were demoralized and divided into a group of machine bosses on the one hand and a handful of insurgent challengers on the other. The insurgents were convinced that the only way they could beat the Democrats in November would be to throw off the yoke of their own political bosses and present the people with a reform ticket. They hired Safire to run a primary campaign for them to uproot the entrenched party bosses.

This was my first exposure to politics and it was a fascinating one. Safire had me do the basic research, take soundings of the situation, and report back to him. I went up to Essex County, interviewed people from all walks of life; I reported to him that there was a great deal of resentment among voters toward one of the Republican party bosses in particular, an individual named Henry Blank. Blank rarely showed up in public and yet he wielded tremendous influence behind the scenes.

When I made my report to Safire he listened intently, asked a few questions. Then he stood up and began the familiar pacing back and forth, humming off-key. I refrained from saying anything because I knew that Bill was intensively thinking the problem through. After 15 minutes or so the humming stopped. Bill was ready. "Here's our strategy. We're going to do a campaign that in essence says 'Beat Boss Blank.' That will be our slogan. We'll make up 'Beat Boss Blank' posters and have them plastered on billboards, on highways, in store windows all over the place. We'll show a face that's nothing but a blob of white space. Everywhere people are going to see a blank face without any eyes, nose, lips. We'll make charges of absentee management; talk about behind-the-scenes manipulation of a boss who presents a faceless facade to the public!"

As I took notes furiously Safire outlined the strategy we would use to implement our campaign. It turned out to be—down to the most minute point—the strategy we actually used. This not only won the primary election overwhelmingly for our reform candidates, overthrowing Boss Blank and his machine, but it enabled the reform Republicans to capture the general election in the fall against their Democratic opponents. Twenty-two reform candidates were elected. As a result of this upheaval, New Jersey was turned into a Nixon state the following year, giving him the vitally needed electoral votes. His race against Humphrey proved to be a close one. New Jersey was a pivotal state. I don't think it's too much to say that the Safire strategy for beating Boss Blank played a major role in putting Nixon in the White House.

During this political campaign I had two close calls that almost ended my career. One day I stepped out of headquarters at the Robert Treat Hotel in Newark when gunfire suddenly exploded. A band of people were milling around shooting bullets into the air. I sneaked into the lot where my car was parked, slammed my foot down on the gas pedal, raced through a red light and sped through side streets and alleys, avoiding the main streets in an effort to get as far away from the gunfire as possible. I barely got out of Newark with my skin intact. I had been caught in the historic Newark riots of 1967 as violence erupted in the black ghettos of major cities across the country.

On another occasion during the campaign I was scheduled to make an important presentation to the reform Republicans who had hired us. While driving to Essex County my car was hit head-on by a truck. It rolled on its side, smashed to smithereens. As I lay in the emergency room at Lenox Hill Hospital, in stormed Bill Safire. I have no idea how he learned of my accident. He couldn't have cared less about the meeting that was scheduled in New Jersey, or that it was extremely important for him to be present. Nor did he care about the political campaign. He paced back and forth muttering, "Who's in charge here. Has Art been X-rayed yet? Where's the nurse? There are cuts on his forehead; why isn't anything being done about them?" The interns and nurses had no idea who Safire was but he exuded such an air of authority he had the entire medical staff running around doing his bidding. In no time I was wheeled into the X-ray room; pictures were taken. All the while Bill stood over me muttering, "Don't worry, you just be all right."

Miraculously, I came out of my ordeal with only a few bruises. I suffered only a mild concussion, although I had been knocked unconscious and my car had been demolished. I stayed overnight in the hospital for observation; after taking a few tests, they let me go. I remained at home for three or four days nursing some aches and a minor whiplash. I emerged from the experience with a permanent affection for Safire for I had discovered that his sometimes brusque exterior concealed a concerned, caring person. That message came through loud and clear.

When Nixon won the election in 1968 Safire was invited by the President-elect to join him in the White House. I became president of his firm and several years later started my own. Although our career paths took us in different directions, Safire and I have remained friends. Besides being a great wordsmith, he is a humansmith par excellence.

CHAPTER SEVEN

ROY COHN: MASTER OF THE CONTROVERSIAL STYLE

Some people always seem to be embroiled in controversy. Fewer people make their taste for controversy the basis of a personal and professional PR program. It is the rare person indeed who can function matter-of-factly in the midst of strife, apparently teetering on the brink of disaster, yet always come out on top.

Roy Cohn, a chapter in anybody's book, is a genius at using public relations as an adjunct to his innate brilliance and his combative personality. As a lawyer he has not only overcome his reputation as a no-holds-barred gutter fighter, he has turned that reputation into a powerful advantage. "When a client is in deep trouble, he wants a no-holds-barred attorney who will never give up the fight for him," says Cohn. His rough, un-yielding approach and his affinity for taking the unpopular side of an argument have brought him fame (some would say notoriety) and many clients.

Cohn first entered the limelight as a member of the govern-ment team that successfully prosecuted Julius and Ethel Rosenberg in the history-making atom spy trial of the early 1950s. Not long afterward he became highly visible as the brash young attorney for the communist-hunting Senator Joseph McCarthy.

Shortly after I started my own business I was retained by Roy Cohn. This was the beginning of a stimulating and challenging relationship.

Riding a Coney Island roller coaster is a tranquilizing experience compared to working with Cohn. I was always on call, prepared to toil round the clock, since he would phone me at any hour and from anywhere he happened to be. Roy was—and is—an obsessive globe-trotter. He took his work with him—to Paris, Acapulco, St. Moritz, the Riviera, Tokyo. And he invariably ended up next to a telephone, pouncing on me with a new command, directive, and insight into the strategy we were devising for a campaign.

Cohn lived beyond the realm of the conventional. He was continually doing things to shock people. When I first started working with him, he asked me to meet him aboard his yacht—a vessel he had bought from Malcolm Forbes, the financial publisher, and christened, appropriately enough, *Defiance*.

I met Roy at the yacht basin on the West Side of Manhattan and we went aboard to discuss business. Roy was in his bathing suit. The crew cast off and we began sailing down the Hudson River. We had gone only a short distance when Roy abruptly broke off our discussion. "Art, excuse me for a moment." He disappeared below deck and emerged with a pair of water skis. He lowered himself into the water, and, as I looked on in amazement, began to ski. I have never seen anybody else water-ski on the Hudson River within a stone's throw of Manhattan's skyscrapers, nor do I believe I will ever again. But this is vintage Roy Cohn. After 10 or 15 minutes he returned to the yacht and we picked up our discussion where we had left off. Cohn's unspoken message was that he did what he wanted to do, whenever and wherever he wished.

On another occasion, in the middle of our battle with the bigwigs of a Texas insurance empire, Roy convened a meeting in his hotel room in Dallas. He summoned a group of distinguished lawyers, business executives, and other powerful men in the state. The conference had been called for early morning. I was the first to arrive and Roy asked me to greet the visitors while he took a quick shower. When our guests appeared Roy hadn't yet emerged. We sipped our coffee and chatted as we waited for him.

Suddenly he entered the room dressed only in a bath towel. He went around the room casually shaking hands with each astounded guest. Then he took a seat and said, "Gentlemen, let's begin business." And he continued to dry himself off as the discussion proceeded.

The case that brought Cohn to me was as bizarre as my client himself. He phoned one morning and invited me to come over. I found Roy, an indefatigable sun worshiper, on the roof of his town house sitting in a lounge chair in a bathing suit. He sports a deep tan year-round. Even during a January blizzard he looks as if he has just stepped off a plane from the Virgin Islands, which is entirely possible.

Cohn opened a file and began outlining to me a case he was then involved in. He was convinced that it required public relations handling if he were to be successful. The case involved Shearn Moody, Jr., the grandson of Texas multimillionaire W. L. Moody, who had amassed a fortune that was enormous even by Texas standards. The senior Moody had founded American National Insurance Company, which became the ninth largest insurance firm in the United States. Upon grandfather Moody's death, his will, calling for the establishment of a Moody Foundation, was dutifully carried out by his heirs. The Foundation was structured so as to dispense monies to social causes in Texas. A more important fact was that the Foundation owned 68.8 percent of American National Insurance company; thus, whoever controlled the Moody Foundation controlled the $1.4 billion assets of American National.

According to the terms of Moody's will, the trustees of the Foundation were to be his grandsons, Shearn and Robert, and his sister Mary. Shearn and Robert were in their early twenties when handed this enormous power. Both were playboys, not the slightest bit interested in business. Powerful outside groups complained that the three members of the Moody family, who constituted the Board of Governors, should not be permitted to control the assets of an insurance company, and they pressured the Texas Legislature into passing a law to increase the board from three to seven, with the purpose of placing on it four non-family members who, by possessing the majority vote, could keep the Moodys from exercising control. In retaliation, Shearn Moody turned to a man he recognized could give vigorous battle to the newly entrenched power clique—Roy Cohn, the New York attorney.

Roy hired my firm to handle the public relations aspects of his campaign on behalf of Shearn Moody. To prepare for my assignment I did a thorough job of researching the history and background of the controversial Moody family. The founder of the fortune, W. L., was a high-handed patriarch who had died just before reaching 90, leaving over a quarter of a billion dollars. Moody, Sr., was outrageously eccentric. He appointed his 19-year-old son president of a bank he owned. When reporters discovered that the youth was the youngest bank president in America and requested a photograph to print in the newspaper, old Moody sent them a picture showing his son at the tender age of seven. To have made a new, up-to-date picture would have cost money and Moody was brought up, he explained, not to squander cash.

Father and son, both strong-willed individuals, wrangled bitterly for years. It didn't help that the boy displayed greater vision than his sire. When, before the First World War, Moody, Sr., discovered that his son had loaned $5,000 to a movie theater owner to buy an organ to play background music for the silent films he was exhibiting, the father flew into a rage. Movies were a temporary fad that would die out any month now, he exploded, and organs belonged in cathedrals, not film houses.

The father-son feud continued to the bitter end. When the older man was in his eighties and his son was in his fifties, Moody, Sr., administered the *coup de grace*. He wrote his son a curt letter suggesting he resign from all of his posts in the Moody empire, and when the younger Moody demurred, he abruptly fired him. He never spoke another word to his son.

In doing battle on behalf of Shearn Moody, Roy Cohn keenly appreciated the role that the press could play. Roy owes a good deal of his success, as well as his notoriety, to conducting his trials by headline. He has an uncanny knowledge of what constitutes a rattling good newspaper story. And because he has so carefully nurtured his contacts with editors and reporters he has received a strikingly fair shake from the media.

Applying the principle that the best defense is a crushing offense, Roy Cohn announced he was filing a $610 million lawsuit on behalf of the great-grandson of W. L. Moody and other stockholders against American National Insurance Company, the Board of Governors of the Foundation, and top officials of the insurance firm. (This $610 million worth of damages represented the market value of all the common stock held in American National Insurance Company.)

Multimillion dollar lawsuits invariably grab newspaper headlines, whether or not they're justified. Announce a big lawsuit and you will get instant media coverage. Anyone at all can file a lawsuit for any amount of money, but if you file one for $50 or $10,000, the media will take little notice of you. File one for $150 million and court reporters, going through the daily legal notices, will phone their editors pronto. Often the figures used in a lawsuit are, to put it bluntly, picked out of a hat. The higher your figure, the more the media will be disposed to believe you have an extremely important complaint to air.

Most such suits are quietly dropped or thrown out of court. But the main objective has been achieved—headlines have been gained for one's cause and the impression has effectively been made that if a plaintiff files a multimillion dollar lawsuit he must have an eminently just cause. This is a technique that Roy Cohn has used over and over again. America is a litigation-happy society.

Bear in mind that the Moody family was not popular with the Texas public. It represented big wealth, overweening power. The community is always for an underdog. The case against the Moody family was overwhelming as far as public sentiment was concerned. But in representing a Moody, we were faced with a stiff, uphill battle.

In working out the tactic of hitting the management of American National Insurance with a $610 million derivative class action stockholder suit, Cohn and I appreciated that this was only a first step. The battle would be a long, arduous one and we would need the support of as many members of the Texas State Legislature as we could get. The legislation which expanded the Board of Trustees had caused the crisis, and the outcome of the struggle would be heavily influenced by legislative action. Cohn hired a corps of investigative researchers to try to uncover the Achilles heel in our opponent's position and we came up with evidence suggesting questionable investment decisions by the top management of American National Insurance Company.

A special subcommittee of the Texas House of Representatives had been established to investigate the activities of major Texas foundations. Our aim, through the use of purposeful public relations, was to focus this investigation on the activities of a single foundation—the Moody's—which was now being administered by the four opponents of the family. Our plan called for Roy Cohn to appear as a witness before the subcommittee. My job was to write a statement and arrange a press conference at the State Capitol in Austin to warm up the press corps.

Cohn is a celebrity wherever he goes. He knows and uses this to the utmost advantage. When he makes a statement, he counts on getting full press attention. Roy was relying on me to write the scenario that would publicly reveal those questionable decisions by top management of the insurance company.

About two weeks before Cohn's scheduled testimony before the Texas House of Representatives' committee, I arranged for facilities in the State Capitol building for our press conference. I sent a telegram to every newspaper, wire service, magazine, radio and television station that had a bureau in Austin. The advantage of holding a press conference in a state capital is that you have a captive group of important press personnel who normally cover legislative happenings. We were certain to have ongoing coverage of our activities by this group. My telegram invited the press to a conference at which I promised that the celebrated attorney, Roy M. Cohn, would make news.

I arrived in Austin two days before the press conference, checked into a hotel near the Capitol building and prepared to warm up my audience before the tornado hit. Austin is a quiet college town, the headquarters of the University of Texas. I walked over to the press room at the Capitol building and spoke with every reporter I was able to get my hands on. Without revealing the precise nature of Cohn's upcoming remarks, I promised them a good show—the kind of show only Cohn could provide.

I was performing what is referred to in political circles as advance work. Despite wariness, each reporter felt obliged to attend the conference. They recognized that news was in the making because Cohn always made news. This was his first visit to Texas and his name was sacrosanct in conservative circles.

The day of the press conference arrived. The room was jam-packed. TV crews from all the major cities in Texas were there in abundance, as were the daily major newspaper reporters. When Cohn walked into the room, I felt as though we were holding a presidential news conference.

Using prepared slides and a quiet, disarming tone which built toward a crescendo, Cohn unveiled a story of family control being spirited away from the Moodys by powerful outside forces who now controlled the American National Insurance Company. He pointed to documents he had uncovered and to various and sundry classified records. He outlined instance after instance of abuse of the public trust. Immediately following the press conference all hell broke loose. Reporters bolted from the room toward the nearest telephones as if they had just learned Texas had seceded from the Union. During the next 24 hours every newspaper in Texas featured the press conference on page one with such banner headlines as "Cohn Cites Abuses in Moody Foundation."

Cohn and his corps of investigators had done a thorough job and many of his charges were subsequently substantiated. The press all over the nation took up the cudgels. Thirty top officers and directors of American National were abruptly thrown on the defensive.

Cohn's campaign had taken on the momentum of a blitz; it had caught our opponents totally off guard. To use the analogy of the World Series, hardly had the contest started when we found ourselves already ahead three games to nothing. The battle dragged on for a couple of years, true enough, but Cohn's opponents were never able to recover. The number of outside directors was reduced and the Moody family regained control of the foundation.

In addition to being an astute courtroom lawyer, Cohn understands how to use public relations techniques to further his interests. He thrives on controversy. "When you're controversial," he points out, "that makes you newsworthy and it further helps to be involved with other controversial people. I'm also a very political animal and that creates more controversy."

Roy Cohn's career is vivid proof of the importance of understanding the dynamics of public perception and how it can be influenced. His use of those dynamics has been, seemingly, diametrically opposed to the precepts of Dale Carnegie, author of *How to Win Friends and Influence People*. Nevertheless, Cohn can be considerate, thoughtful, and cooperative; he knows the importance of these characteristics, too.

One of Cohn's long-time adversaries has been Ken Auletta, a political writer. Auletta has written articles labeling Cohn a mean, tough guy. Cohn never fails to thank Auletta for this publicity. Once he wrote a letter saying, "Dear Ken, I want to drop you a note to thank you. A mention from you is always something which elevates my importance in the profession and in the public eye."

The basic strategy for successful PR, he points out, is to cultivate friendships with key editors and reporters. Cohn boasts of 30 years worth of friendships with news people. And although he is a notorious conservative in his political outlook, he has not confined his friendships to newsmen who share his conservative ideology. "Everyone would expect me to be friendly with William F. Buckley, Jr., and Richard Viguerie, but people are very much surprised when they know that I am equally friendly with Marty Peretz of the *New Republic* and Mort Zuckerman of the *Atlantic,* or that I return phone calls from the *Village Voice,* although a lot of my conservative colleagues do not." In short, it is one of Cohn's basic tenets that he will talk to any newspaperman who calls him. "I will always return calls. I do not know of any story that can't be made better by talking to a reporter and answering his questions."

UPI / BETTMANN NEWSPHOTOS

Roy Cohn is master of the controversial style. He is a genius at using public relations to present his clients' views through the media. One of his memorable teachers was the late Senator Joseph McCarthy who taught Cohn how to attract media attention.

CHAPTER EIGHT

FROM RIALTO TO REAL ESTATE: PR HITS AND BOMBS

Mastery of the principles of public relations underlies a diversity of successful careers today.

We expect PR to play a large role in show business, and indeed it does. My fascination with show business is, in fact, one reason why I wound up in PR.

My first love was the theater. I attended the High School of Performing Arts in New York—breeding ground for so many stars and locale for the movie and TV show *Fame*—and studied theater. While I later concluded that stardom on the stage was probably not for me, I have, I believe, been able to put some of my theatrical bent to work in public relations.

When Bill Safire offered me a job I took it primarily because of one account. Safire had just signed to represent the League of New York Theaters. This would give me a chance to work with producers like David Merrick, Hal Prince, and Alexander Cohen, and to help promote Broadway.

One of the most significant things we did for the League was to transform the Tony Awards. At that time the awards were distributed at a cocktail party, with perhaps some local TV coverage. Safire suggested that they should be on network TV, a big event, equivalent to the Academy Award "Oscar" ceremonies.

Safire made his case persuasively, pacing back and forth before the producers in his characteristic way. When he finished there was a pause. Then David Merrick said, "Bill, it sounds good, but no TV network is going to be interested in these minor awards."

Safire looked him in the eye and retorted, "Awards are minor or major, depending on the eye of the beholder."

"I'll bet anyone here," rejoined Merrick, "that next year the awards will be presented at a little cocktail party the same as this year."

Safire said, "You're on."

We made the rounds of the networks. The Tony Awards were bought as a network special. The rest is history.

Two of Broadway's most successful producers, Morton Gottlieb and Alexander H. Cohen, are masters in the use of PR strategies. Gottlieb is the producer of such hits as *Sleuth*, *Same Time Next Year*, and *Tribute*. He has been so skillful in using public relations that he has been able to obliterate the negative publicity of bad or lukewarm reviews for some of his productions. It is conventional wisdom on Broadway that bad reviews can kill a play, yet Gottlieb has shown time and again how to nullify the impact of bad reviews by using cleverly conceived publicity.

Gottlieb worked himself up from press agent to company manager and finally to Broadway producer. When he presented the play *Tribute*, starring Jack Lemmon, he arranged for an opening night party at the Tavern On The Green. Gottlieb was preparing an announcement that he knew would grab headlines in *Variety*. He was prepared, during the party festivities on opening night, to hand each of the show's investors a check paying back their investment in full. The idea of a producer paying his investors back their entire investment on opening night was unheard-of. But Gottlieb had succeeded in making enough money during the out-of-town tryouts to be willing to break precedent. Came opening night, Gottlieb had the checks ready to hand out when he was given a copy of *The New York Times*, fresh from the presses, carrying a review of his play. The notice panned it savagely. Someone handed Gottlieb a review from the *Daily News* that was equally hostile. He became nervous; should he take the chance and pass out money to his investors when the play had already received two negative reviews? It could fold in a week. He thought it over and decided he would take the risk and hand out the money. The afternoon newspapers gave abundant coverage to the news of his unprecedented action and it helped take the sting out of the bad reviews the play otherwise received. *Tribute* survived and went on to become a hit.

Gottlieb remains a spectacular believer in getting newspaper space through publicity stunts, rather than paying for advertising. Once he's launched a hit the trick is to keep it running indefinitely. When a Gottlieb play has completed three years, this maestro of publicity devises ingenious stunts for keeping it going for a fourth year. He had a succession of stars take over the two lead roles in *Same Time Next Year*. When Sandy Dennis assumed the role, Gottlieb took advantage of the fact that she was a cat-lover who kept a menage of 42 pets. He contacted an organization which specialized in finding new homes for kittens—Bide-A-Wee. In the morning before one matinee performance, he arranged a cat auction in the theater lobby. He put a number of animals from Bide-A-Wee on display for a couple of days before the auction was held for anyone who wished to make an offer. Sandy Dennis was photographed accepting the bids. Coffee and donuts were served to everyone who attended. The event was widely covered by television, and ended in time to make the evening newspapers.

When Hope Lange took over Sandy's role in the show and Gottlieb found out she was a dog lover, he held a dog auction, garnering wide publicity for the city's stray canines.

Gottlieb has made daring use of public relations to create stars. In his early years as general manager for Gilbert Miller, the producer was planning to do a play called *Gigi*, adapted from a story by Colette. The company looked far and wide for a big-name star to play the lead. A number of candidates were considered. Leslie Caron was one, but it was decided that her thick French accent would make her too difficult to understand. Finally, Gottlieb and his colleagues decided to hire a relatively unknown girl. They selected Audrey Hepburn who, while she had done bit roles in a couple of movies and had been in the chorus of several musicals, had never before spoken a line of dialogue on the stage. "We were determined," Gottlieb recalled, "to make Audrey Hepburn a star overnight. We planned to do this with a barrage of publicity, helped, we hoped, by rave reviews of her performance. However, when the play opened it didn't get the reviews that Audrey needed to become an instant star. The reviews were only lukewarm."

Fortunately, Gottlieb had already sold seven weeks of theater parties in advance, which assured that business would be coming in for that period of time no matter what. "There was nothing left for us to do but go ahead anyway and make Audrey the star we had predicted she would become." He arranged for Hepburn to be photographed standing under the theater marquee while her name was given star billing. Ads were run with the phrase, "Star bright." Gottlieb had already prepared all the publicity before opening night describing how Audrey had become a superstar. Now all that was necessary was to give it to the press, and the press accepted it because Gottlieb and his colleagues fortunately had enough money in the till to guarantee a seven-weeks' run of the show no matter what happened.

As a result, newspaper editors and especially the editors of *Life* and *Look*, which came out weekly, knew that the show would be around for at least seven weeks and that if they ran

Gottlieb's publicity releases they wouldn't look foolish by having the show fold overnight. So *Life* and *Look* ran cover photos and stories on Audrey Hepburn and reams of print on how she had risen to stardom. The public, reading about how a new star had been born, flocked to the theater to see and applaud her. In the process Hepburn actually *became* the star that Gottlieb had promised. It was a striking case of publicity forcing the confirmation of the very claims it was making, turning the promotion into fact. Hepburn, of course, had star potential and would have made it anyway sooner or later, but Gottlieb's publicity certainly hastened matters along.

Skillful use of public relations can enormously facilitate one's ability to receive important financing in the real estate field. There is a story that a businessman who urgently needed a loan went to one of the original Rothschilds. Rothschild explained that he wouldn't give him the money directly but would offer him something equally as good. "Meet me tomorrow on the floor of the London Stock Exchange. We will walk across it together. When my bankers see me with my arm around you, you'll get from them all the financing you need."

New Yorker Donald Trump is not only a multimillionaire real estate tycoon, but a much-photographed, much-ballyhooed personality. He has made the transition from a successful real estate operator to a media superstar. And this has been done through the skillful use of public relations.

Trump's father, Fred, started out as an assistant to a carpenter, went into real estate and made a fortune building apartments in Queens and Brooklyn. Upon joining his father's firm, Donald expanded the business into Manhattan and by his mid-thirties had transformed much of the Big Apple's landscape. He has revitalized the area around Grand Central Station by turning the venerable old Commodore Hotel into the spanking new Grand Hyatt, a marvel of modern design and engineering. He has put up one of the world's flashiest and most expensive condominium buildings, Trump Tower—a $100 million edifice consisting of 40 floors of luxury apartments, some with lavish swimming pools and all with bathrooms lined in marble, offering whirlpool baths. The apartments have been sold for up to $10 million. He has also built the world's largest casino, in Atlantic City, and has moved into the sports world, buying the New Jersey Generals, the flagship team of the new United States Football League.

Trump is a master at getting publicity, but it wasn't always that way. When I first met him he hardly knew the difference between a press photographer and a hedgehog. He was a young man working for his father in Brooklyn. The U.S. Justice Department, beset by pressure from minority groups, came up with the charge that the Trumps were refusing to rent to black families in their housing projects. The Trumps denied this, claiming they were being made a scapegoat by political forces. Donald Trump met Cohn at a party and mentioned his troubles to him. Cohn took him on as a client and turned to me to provide help.

Anybody accused of discrimination in housing was *ipso facto* condemned by much of the public in those days, even before he had a chance to plead his case in court. The attitude in New York City was especially hostile to landlords. It was my job to take this negative publicity and turn it into positive publicity for Trump.

Roy Cohn advised Trump to fight fire with fire. He told Trump, "We're going to sue the United States Justice Department for libeling you when they charge you with discriminating against blacks. We'll file a $150 million slander suit." I called a press conference with the assurance that the room would be jammed with the New York press and television representatives. For a private citizen to file a suit against the United States Justice Department was a sensational move. Imagine a citizen turning the tables on the Washington bureaucracy!

It was Donald Trump's first press conference and he was nervous when he took the floor. But I had rehearsed him thoroughly and he really got going. He painted a picture of flagrant injustice, charging that the Trumps were being made a scapegoat. He and his father, he said, were not guilty of discrimination against minority groups but were themselves the victims of discrimination by the government to appease powerful vested interests.

Trump received dramatic headlines. He was propelled in one fell swoop from obscurity to national recognition. Our $150 million lawsuit against the Justice Department never came to trial. It wasn't designed to. A compromise was worked out quietly. The Justice Department dropped its charges and Trump dropped his slander suit. These events didn't make news, they were buried in the court files. What stayed alive in the minds of people was that Trump had filed a multimillion-dollar lawsuit against the Department of Justice. People everywhere asked admiringly, "Who is this young man with such chutzpah?"

When Donald Trump saw the national attention he got as a result of his news conference he was flabbergasted. He had never realized what power the media could wield. He awoke to the fact that one could get an awful lot of mileage out of headlines that could promote his business ventures, if he created news the press would be interested in.

Steadily Trump became a name to reckon with, not only in New York, but around the country. And, indeed, out of his brilliant real estate mind came many truly workable ideas— one for a new convention center, another for a new hotel, the Grand Hyatt. He became the subject of articles in *Business Week*, *Fortune*, *The New York Times*, *Time*, *Newsweek*. As a result of this publicity he began to be taken more and more seriously. His new-found fame helped earn him the respect of his seniors and persuaded them that his vision of a revitalized New York was worth taking seriously. He brought to fruition many revolutionary projects that are now a matter of record. And all this while he was still in his thirties.

PR exposure helped Trump establish the number-one thing needed by a real estate executive—credibility with the public.

Today Trump is very well known. News people now pursue him. He has become his own master publicity agent and he has moved into areas beyond the real estate field.

We assume that politicians are adept at public relations. Some, however, show surprising maladroitness.

Veteran TV newsman Gabe Pressman recalls that when John V. Lindsay was mayor of New York, he got along wonderfully with the publisher of *The New York Times*, with whom he broke bread frequently, but that he was strongly disliked by the reporters on *the Times* and other New York newspapers because of his aloofness. Lindsay tried to repair his standing with reporters by reassigning his press secretary and bringing in a new man, Harry O'Donnell. The first thing Harry did was to announce a ribbon-cutting ceremony at which the Mayor would be available to be interviewed by the press. As long as Pressman could recall there had been a men's room in the Mayor's section of City Hall. On Lindsay's order it had been closed off to news reporters. Now Harry O'Donnell held his press conference for the sole purpose of announcing that the men's room had been reopened for the use of reporters. All they had to do, he announced, was to press a buzzer and go through the gate to reach it without any red tape. "Harry had a ribbon-cutting ceremony simply to reopen the men's room. It was a very inside joke, not one of great public interest, but the way Harry handled it inaugurated a new era of press relations in the Lindsay Administration," Pressman reports.

Pressman recalls that at the height of the separatist movement in Canada, when Quebec elected a Prime Minister on a platform of secession, he tried to interview the new P.M., Rene Levesque, as he was arriving for a reception at a New York hotel. Just as Pressman was starting to say, "Mr. Prime Minister," a member of the Canadian's party got behind him, tripped him, and sent him sprawling on his back while his cameraman continued to take pictures. In trying to keep his balance as he fell, Pressman clutched at the bodyguard who had pushed him and was amazed to discover as he lay on the floor that he was holding a gold watch belonging to his assailant. It was impossible to return it to its owner because the Prime Minister's party had gone into the ballroom for the reception. Pressman got on the air, told of the incident, and concluded, "I'd like to return the guy's watch if he'd please step forward." Needless to say, no one appeared. Pressman approached the Watchmaker's Association to have the valuable gold watch traced, but they were unable to find the owner.

One of America's most notorious PR buffs is Mayor Koch of New York. The Mayor could give lessons on the nuances of promoting oneself, and yet even His Honor has blundered on occasion in his handling of the media. Pressman related how once, after making critical remarks about the Mayor on his television show, he received a nasty letter from His Honor, demanding the right to appear on the airwaves and answer him. Pressman replied in a letter that was brief and to the point. "You're full of shit, Mr. Mayor. You don't have any more right to be on our airwaves than I or any other reporter has the right to sound off in the Blue Room [the Mayor's executive office]. Best Wishes for the New Year."

In short, a wise PR man doesn't try to manipulate the press.

Sometimes an urge to publicize oneself lurks in the most unexpected quarters. Pressman has devoted much of his time to investigating leaders of the underworld. He recalls how one day he came with his cameraman to cover New York mobster Joey Gallo, who, flanked by his lawyers, was on his way to a Grand Jury. It was unheard of for a gangster to talk to the press. Even if he were so inclined, his lawyers would shut him up. Nevertheless, Pressman tried his luck. "Joey, can I talk to you?" "Sure, sure, any time." Then his lawyer burst in, "Shut up, Joey. Don't say a word to him!" They were walking along the corridor leading to the Grand Jury room. Pressman's cameraman had his lens focused on him. Pressman shot out, "What about those guns they found in your club-house, Joey?" And the gangster replied, "Well, I've got a hunting lodge up in the Adirondacks. I use the guns for hunting game up there."

This gangster had such a compulsive need to publicize himself that he threw caution to the winds. He went on trial, received a 10-year jail sentence, and as he emerged from the courtroom handcuffed to guards, spotted Pressman again and exclaimed, "Well, if it ain't my favorite television reporter." "Joey," Pressman asked, "are you bitter about your sentence?" "No, I understand it," replied the gangster who displayed such a keen sense of public relations. "After all, this is an election year." Gallo's need for publicity to satisfy his insatiable ego ended in disaster. His underworld colleagues, furious at his loose tongue, assassinated him.

CHAPTER NINE

PR
And the
Scales of
Justice

This is the story of a PR campaign devoted to a highly unusual purpose . . . the use of public relations strategy in helping to free a man who had been convicted of murder, spent 10 years in a state penitentiary, and who had lost all hope of release. I am as proud of this campaign as of anything I have ever undertaken.

It happened about five years after I had founded my own firm. I was approached by the family of the young man who had been convicted of the crime. My review of the case persuaded me there had been a miscarriage of justice. But what could be done?

While the basic facts are as I present them here, I've disguised some of the circumstances and withheld the young man's name.

The man received a second degree conviction and was sentenced from 20 years to life. He was the scion of a wealthy family and the case had received wide attention in the press.

The defendant's father, convinced his son was innocent, spent a million dollars on lawyers, using every possible legal maneuver to get him out of prison. Some of the most celebrated criminal lawyers in the country were hired, among them F. Lee Bailey and Louis Nizer. One by one they filed briefs, went to court, and were turned down. Louis Nizer handled one appeal, presenting evidence indicating that it was impossible for the defendant to have committed the crime he was convicted of. But the Court of Appeals upheld the original jury conviction.

After 10 years of fruitless effort, the father, as a last resort, turned to my public relations firm to get the story out to the public. The cause I was asked to represent was a highly unusual one for a public relations counsel. But all legal efforts to reverse the verdict had failed. I was called in because the family felt it had to go beyond legal channels and stir up a public demand for their son's release.

Before I took on the client I had to be convinced there was a reasonable basis for concluding the wrong person had been sent to jail. I thoroughly reviewed the trial testimony, the appeals, and the evidence. Although I was a layman and had no knowledge of the legal intricacies of the situation, I had the gut feeling that an innocent man had been convicted. To further satisfy myself, I visited the federal penitentiary where the prisoner was confined. I met and talked with him.

The defendant's trial, I became convinced, had been rife with dubious procedures. Key witnesses who could have shown that the defendant was somewhere else at the time of the murder were barred by the judge from testifying. Witnesses had lied at the Grand Jury inquest and had changed their testimony at the trial. During the trial the family had gotten very bad advice from their lawyer; they were told not to cooperate with the press. Every time news photographers tried to snap pictures of the defendant and other family members they had covered their faces with a newspaper. They presented the worst possible image to the public.

Traditionally, lawyers have advised their clients not to talk to the press. This has been considered by the legal profession to be the safest procedure. Only recently have attorneys appreciated that the media, far from being an implacable foe, can in many cases be of tremendous help. If a defendant has nothing to conceal it is to his benefit to be open with the press. Nowadays, astute lawyers are not only allowing their clients to talk to newsmen, they themselves will talk at length to them. But the family of my client took the advice of an old-school attorney to shun publicity and it certainly didn't help their cause.

I realized that I had quite a job on my hands, since the state had looked upon the prosecution of my client as a milestone case with major political implications. The defendant was a son of a wealthy businessman. The prosecution had been out to show that in a city of oppressed minorities a rich white man would be treated no differently from the black or Hispanic charged with a crime. The family of the defendant contended that he had been made a scapegoat by the politically ambitious district attorney because he was wealthy. If he had been a member of a minority group, they claimed, the case would have been given no prominence and would have been buried on the back pages.

In taking on the assignment I wrote the defendant's father a memo making clear what I conceived my job to be. "The work I do in no way presents a conflict to attorneys. I file no briefs; I make no motions. My job is to create attention, gain support. If I do my job well, and I've no reason to think otherwise, then a creative attorney can work with me to take advantage of the ammunition I am able to bring him during the course of my program. Needless to say, I am well aware of what is involved in this matter; I do not take this assignment lightly."

I had become convinced that if I could generate enough of a ground swell of public opinion, it would force the elected officials to take action. If there was enough insistence by the media and the public that an injustice had been perpetrated, something eventually would have to be done by the governor of the state, who was beholden to public opinion.

But I was faced with a formidable challenge. The murder, the trial, and the conviction of my client had taken place more than 10 years earlier. As a news story it had died long ago. I had the problem of approaching the newspapers with a warmed-over story and persuading them to revive it. Moreover, I had to find ways of keeping it alive and fresh in the minds of the press and the public for the long months it might take to get political action.

It is difficult for a public relations man to keep a story alive when every 24 hours a new event captures the world's attention. It's one thing to place a breaking story in the newspaper. It's another thing to sustain a continuing story day after day, week after week, month after month, and to generate continuing publicity for it.

My strategy from the outset was to avoid one-shot roll-outs, especially press conferences. The use of a press conference is important when one has a really major news development to report, such as when we announced that Donald Trump was filing his $150 million lawsuit against the Justice Department. You get a lot of attention all at once; then it's over. I realized that in this case if I held a press conference I would get the news out all at once and I would be unable to sustain it in the weeks and months of fighting that lay ahead. My strategy for sustaining news over a period of time is to custom-tailor different themes and subsidiary lines on the story for different media outlets. I would go to *Time* magazine with one idea for an article, then go with variations on the subject to the *Today* and *Good Morning America* shows. I would balance the monthly magazines with the daily newspapers, the radio with the television shows. I would generate an ongoing array of every possible type of media exposure.

I assigned three of the top writers in my firm to work with me on this project. But first I felt they had to be as convinced as I was of the worthiness of the cause. I told them I wouldn't ask them to collaborate if they had any reservations about our client's innocence. When I received assurances from them that they didn't, I put them to work.

I drew up a timetable of six to eight months to sustain publicity, geared to build momentum so that it would reach a climax just before Christmas, which was the traditional time for state governors to consider commuting prison sentences. I decided to open up full throttle on this aspect. There was the prisoner himself, the young man who, I charged, was discriminated against precisely because he was rich and did not qualify for the solicitude often shown by the authorities toward the poor and underprivileged. I prepared releases and editorial memoranda to leading editors, TV news people, magazine writers, and columnists, pointing out how the impact of my client's confinement spread far beyond his prison cell; how his father, now 71 years old, had spent every waking moment of the last 10 years attempting to prove his son's innocence. I suggested to editors and feature columnists the opportunity of doing interviews and stories with the prisoner's sister, who would tell how she had dealt with the disaster of having a brother in prison on a murder conviction. I made the father, the mother, the sisters and brothers available to TV reporters and newspaper writers. They described how their lives had been affected by the tragedy. They told of their anguish at having friends they had known for years suddenly turn their backs on them when they found out who the convict was. We managed to enlist a high-ranking prelate of the Catholic hierarchy in our campaign. I got the monsignor wide coverage in the press. He went on one television show after another to discuss his belief in my client's innocence and the injustice that he felt had been done him.

In short order, the story of my client and his family became front page news, not only in New York, but across the country. Columnists from coast to coast featured the case; magazine writers followed suit. I kept the story going full blast by tailoring different variations for different media outlets.

My campaign had been designed to generate public awareness and it was successful. Numerous civic and social groups called me to offer their help for the prisoner and his family. Others got up petitions and sent them to the governor. Stirred by this upsurge of public indignation, the governor and other officials in Albany bent over backwards to find an excuse to release my client. He was given a much speedier parole than he would otherwise have been entitled to. The negotiations were conducted by the governor and the family's attorneys. And when my client was released from jail, it was done with no fanfare at all. As far as the politicians were concerned, enough publicity had already been generated by our side. They wanted no more headlines. No official would publicly concede that my client had not been given a fair trial, nor would they concede that perhaps he had been innocent, but because of their acute sensitivity to the electorate and embarrassment at the publicity my client was getting, they found a way for him to be released quickly, so as to remove a thorn in their side.

The press, in America and abroad, took note of the novel role that a public relations campaign had played. Legal experts wrote articles pointing out that this was a rare instance in which a defendant, having been convicted of a crime and exhausting every legal tool available to change the decision, enlisted a public relations firm to whip up popular opinion which helped to reverse an injustice. A writer in the London *Times* interviewed me as an example of a professional who demonstrated dramatically how public relations can and should be used for any proper cause, even though it be an unconventional one.

In recent years there have been other instances in which public relations has been used to reach the public beyond the walls of the courtroom. Undoubtedly, this practice can be abused. Yet there will continue to be cases in which injustices are done and innocent people sent to prison to languish in obscurity.

CHAPTER TEN

POWERS AND LIMITATIONS OF PR

There is nothing more exhilarating than dealing with people, ideas, and power. That's what public relations is all about. It can be frustrating. It can be deeply satisfying. But it is never dull.

It's important to understand the source of the satisfaction.

In the early 1920s Walter Lippmann, the political columnist, wrote a book called *Public Opinion*, which I have read and reread over the years. Lippmann points out that there is very little in the way of objective truth. There are at least two sides to most issues confronting society and it is vitally necessary for any group or individual, when they believe in a cause, to get their message across through public relations. PR, as Bernays has defined it, is "the engineering of public opinion."

There are, of course, limits to what even the most skillful public relations can accomplish. All the PR ingenuity in the world can't prevail against an idea or trend whose time has come. A classic example is the introduction of the automobile in America. When the auto first burst on the scene the horse and carriage industry fought frantically to prevent its acceptance. The "buggy whip" people unleashed a massive public relations campaign in an effort to turn the American people against the automobile. Ministers across the land were called on to denounce the desire of people to drive as an emotional disease—they termed it "automobilitis"—which was destructive to religion and morals. Prodded by lobbyists, the Tennessee State Legislature passed a law requiring anybody who intended to drive an automobile to advertise in the newspapers a week in advance of his outing so as to warn all pedestrians in the area. The campaign of the horse and carriage industry mounted as the auto continued to gain wider acceptance. As the speed of early autos reached the "terrifying" level of 20 miles an hour, public relations specialists paid eminent brain surgeons to issue warnings that motoring would drive people insane. A leading neurosurgeon, Dr. Winslow Forbes, wrote, "When these racing motor cars reach 30 miles an hour, they must drive themselves for no human brain is capable of dealing with all the emergencies that may arise should that rate be maintained for any period worth thinking of. The human animal is simply not destined to travel 30 miles an hour; neither the human brain nor the human eye can keep pace with it." Despite these ringing prophecies of doom, Americans accepted the automobile and it revolutionized our way of life. The public relations barrage launched by the horse and carriage industry was doomed to failure because it was battling the march of industrial progress.

The cleverest public relations in the world cannot successfully promote, for any length of time, a poor cause or a poor product. By contrast, skillful public relations can speed up the acceptance of a concept whose time *has* come. A striking example of this involved eminent public relations consultant Edward Gottlieb. In the early 1950s, when the newly formed State of Israel was struggling for recognition in the court of world opinion, America was largely apathetic. Gottlieb, who at the time headed his own public relations firm, suddenly had a hunch about how to create a more sympathetic attitude toward Israel. He chose a writer and sent him to Israel with instructions to soak in the atmosphere of the country and create a novel about it. The book turned out to be *Exodus*, by Leon Uris. His novel did more to popularize Israel with the American public than any other single presentation through the media. The attention of the public was drawn to the book, and the perception of the public was influenced by its heart-rending account of the flight of refugees from Nazism.

Public relations triumphs do not happen because of manipulation. The myth of the manipulator who plays Svengali to the public was once popular. It's going out of style, but it has by no means disappeared.

This myth of the super-manipulative PR man harms the professional in a number of ways. Clients sometime confuse expertise with omnipotence. They think the PR professional can gain unlimited access to any given page in the newspaper, any magazine, any TV show, simply by using a combination of flattery and expense account lunches.

Some journalists, particularly younger ones, buy the myth also, and react to it with a high level of scorn for PR professionals before they have had the opportunity to work with any of them. Occasionally my first meeting with a young journalist resembles that standard scene in the old western movies in which the eager kid wants to make a name for himself by shooting it out with the veteran gunslinger. Usually I am able to convince the "kid" that I am not there to "shoot it out," or to try to buy coverage. I am there to work with him or her.

In a typical example, some years ago, when I was the young public relations director of Prentice-Hall, the publishing house decided to extend its parking lot. Because this would involve cutting down some trees, some in the community rose up in arms. One reporter from a local paper began to write savage stories about this giant corporation, brutal and heartless, that was going to inflict its will on the community and practically strip-mine the landscape. Furthermore, the stories implied, this was yet another example of how corporate America rapes the land and commits a multitude of sins against humanity.

After much effort I got the reporter to sit down with me at lunch. I did not try to sell my company's point of view directly.

My first objective was to let the reporter get to know me, not as a monster but as a human being, doing his job.

We talked about our jobs, our interests—everything *but* the parking lot issue. At the end of two hours the reporter said, "I have been a little rough on your company, haven't I?" I smiled. "Maybe you have."

A door had opened. The reporter saw that the company was not a massive, impersonal entity, but rather an enterprise made up of human beings, doing their best for themselves and their families. And his coverage began to reflect the fact that there were two sides to the issue. This did not happen because I had pleaded a cause. It happened because we had gotten to know each other.

The reporter learned something. So did I. I learned that the best way to get a person with an *a priori* bias to open his mind is to establish a dialogue. When the other party comes to trust my credibility and integrity, he will listen to what I have to say.

The public relations profession brings you into contact with many illustrious people. You quickly learn that they are all human.

During my stint as PR director for Prentice-Hall, the company entered merger negotiations with RCA. An agreement in principle was reached, and I found myself in a room with the heads of the two companies and the PR people from RCA, trying to work out a press release.

RCA was run by the redoubtable David Sarnoff; Prentice-Hall by Richard Prentice Ettinger. Both were battle-hardened veterans in the latter years of highly successful careers as leaders. Both were tough, crusty, volatile, strong-willed, and dominant. RCA was by far the larger firm, but Ettinger (who was called RPE) was utterly unwilling to be deferential.

As a young guy, not long in his job, I suppose I should have been more awed, maybe a little frightened. Certainly awe and fear were emanating from the other staff people in the room. But on the whole I was exhilarated, tickled pink at seeing history made.

But what I was seeing was not so much history being made as hell being raised. General Sarnoff and RPE were arguing about commas, periods, semicolons, dots, and dashes. General Sarnoff tried to exert his weight, insisting that RCA be mentioned far more often than Prentice-Hall. RPE would have none of it. The General declaimed, "For God's sake, RCA is like Mount Everest, Prentice-Hall is like an anthill!" RPE responded with a suitable insult. They continued to trade barbs. The onlookers were white with tension.

And suddenly I began to laugh. As I laughed uncontrollably, the two titans stopped fighting and turned to look at me balefully. As I laughed, it crossed my mind that they were probably wondering about the last wishes of this suicidal individual on his way to the scaffold. At last RPE asked, forbiddingly, "What is so funny?"

"RPE, General," I replied, "with all due respect, you two are business heroes who have built great communications companies from the ground up. And here you are, arguing about periods and commas instead of talking dollars and cents!"

There was a deathly hush, as if those present were waiting for lightning to strike. Then RPE started to grin. Sarnoff began to grin too. Then he laughed. In a moment, both were laughing. "Art," I was told, "you chose the right field to go into." With the atmosphere lightened we worked out a release.

But it was predictable that the chemistry between the two giants would be less than placid. A few months later the deal fell through.

I recalled this episode not long ago when talk arose of Gulf & Western acquiring Prentice-Hall to join with Simon & Schuster in the formation of a publishing colossus.

There's no greater thrill in our business than getting a favorable article in print or on the air. In fact, there's no greater thrill to most people regardless of what their station in life might be than getting their name in the media. Chief executive officers of Fortune 500 companies beam when they are approached on the golf course after a favorable article has appeared in an important newspaper. "Nice story in the *Wall Street Journal*, Jim." That's all a chief executive officer has to hear and it is during such times that he is most likely to pat his public relations manager on the back.

Public relations people, however, always live in fear of the so-called "hatchet job"—an unfavorable article about a company or organization that seems to be a reporter's way of venting his spleen. Sometimes the hatchet blow is a complete surprise. A reporter and a public relations professional will have a number of discussions about a particular article that is either being planned by the reporter or recommended by the public relations professional. Obviously, the professional is thinking of a favorable and positive story, and it appears that the reporter is taking this approach as well. After all of the preparations and appropriate interviews with company personnel, the public relations professional anticipates a favorable story. Occasionally he will be extremely disappointed with the outcome because it appears that the reporter had planned all along to come down heavily and unfavorably on the company. Word of such a double-cross is quickly passed around through the public relations grapevine to other professionals in companies, agencies, and organizations. That reporter is not to be trusted—stay away from him. I don't mean to suggest that the reporter's career comes to a standstill as a result of this, but he will be treated most warily by public relations professionals and chances are the best stories that public relations professionals want to see or hear in the media will be given to that reporter's competitors. In the long run, reporters who incur the mistrust of public relations people make their jobs much harder. When they attempt to develop articles that require assistance from public relations people, they will be avoided like the plague.

The media, in turn, will steer clear of a public relations professional who distorts the truth. Imagine the chagrin of a financial writer who writes a favorable article about a company and then discovers that there were certain pertinent facts left out of the information given to him—like the fact that the company is going to lose $5 million in the quarter just ending. If you attempt to pull the wool over a reporter's eyes just once, you will not be trusted again.

Within the past few years, a public relations person apparently did something to alienate an editor of the *Washington Post*. The irate editor sent a memorandum to members of her staff insisting they have no further dealings with public relations professionals, and that writers who work for her should bypass public relations sources and go over their heads. This mandate caused quite a stir among PR people and was the lead story in many of the trade newsletters. There was such an outcry over the inherent unfairness of the order that Ben Bradlee, executive editor of the *Post*, had to intercede. He reversed his editor's ruling and made it clear that public relations professionals are a necessary resource for the media. It was a small victory for public relations people in the larger war to encourage the media to trust the profession and work closely with it.

This trust must be earned, however, says Bruce Harrison, president of the Washington, D.C.-based public affairs and public relations firm E. Bruce Harrison Company, who sympathizes with the *Washington Post* editor who attempted to pull the plug on public relations people.

"I can truly understand why media people engage in fits of pique against our field at times. Any public relations professional dealing with the media must do his or her homework on the particular needs of the media. We must do market research and the market we research is media.

"When one of my people tells me that he doesn't want to go back to a newspaper reporter because that reporter is tough to deal with, I respectfully point out that maybe our person hasn't made it a point to find out what the reporter's beat is and what material is called for."

It's been said that one way of defining public relations is to call it the social conscience of the products, services, and causes it represents. This is not far from the truth. The truth is that a public relations professional represents only one side of what may be a multi-sided issue. And your goal as a public relations professional is to influence public opinion so that your client or organization can achieve its purpose. So it is less a question of social consciousness than a matter of advocacy. Because public relations is always trying to sell something, it obviously represents only one side of the issue. It is the job of the media to weigh all of the factors presented to it by all sides and determine which position is more persuasive and logical. I do not envy the public relations professional who might try to convince the media that Libya is led by a model statesman; that heroin is a harmless drug; that communism is the correct form of government for the United States; that air pollution is good for us; and that child pornography should be allowed.

It is true that in our democratic form of government, where all points of view can be discussed, truth and righteousness are likely to prevail. However, there are subtle shadings to what constitutes truth. If a high government official advocates building up our nuclear power to deter future wars, is his the truth? Is his opponent's view that we are wasting our funds on expanding our nuclear arsenal also the truth? We're dealing with highly complex contemporary issues and you can be sure that public relations professionals play an important part in attempting to persuade the public that their view is more correct than the opposing view. Fortunately, free elections and the ballot box ultimately resolve the question of which way the American public wants to go on any given issue.

Pundits will forever debate the issue of how public opinion is formed. Did McCarthyism prevail in the early fifties because the media responded to every pronouncement by the late Senator McCarthy as to how many communists there were in everyone's closet? Or did McCarthy sense that the public was so panicked that it welcomed any steps to remove communists from our society? Could entertainment professionals today be blacklisted and prevented from finding work as they were in the early fifties? Or do we learn from history that the public will be trifled with only so long and then will rise up and change current mores and patterns? If you were a public relations professional representing a blacklisted Hollywood writer 30 years ago, your arguments would probably have fallen on deaf ears. Today your job would be a lot easier.

Clearly, a successful campaign must be attuned to the temper of the times.

Motivation is a mysterious process. It has a dynamic all its own. I've attended a lot of sales meetings, usually to report on PR results and plans. The primary function of many sales meetings is to whip up the troops. Sometimes it is not altogether clear *why* they get so whipped up—but it happens.

I recall a meeting conducted by a Midwestern brush manufacturer—the bristle king, manufacturer of hairbrushes, toothbrushes, clothesbrushes, furniture brushes—you name it.

The sales meeting took place in a hotel ballroom. The climax was to be the announcement of a new product that would revolutionize the marketplace. The sales manager stood at the side of a stage at one end of the ballroom. The stage curtain was closed. A band played. Then there was a hush. The sales manager proclaimed, "All right, men! This is it!" A fanfare from the band. The curtain opened to disclose—a photograph of a haircurler.

The salespeople went crazy. They stood, applauded, whistled, screamed, yelled, sang "God Bless America." I confess that I felt a little out of it, unable to muster the same enthusiasm for a haircurler.

But I say thank God for the sales reps who can and do feel such enthusiasm for any product they sell, even the most mundane. They spark the American system.

Ronald Reagan has demonstrated dramatically that a president who can master the art of television communication can persuade the public to do his bidding. A presidential press conference usually helps to achieve this goal.

CHAPTER ELEVEN

PERSUASION WITHOUT ADVERTISING: PR AND THE PROFESSIONS

Professionals from such disciplines as the law and architecture have made adroit and profitable use of the principles of public relations to build their reputations and enhance their practices.

Physicians have been slower to use PR. But increasing competition in the medical field has led to some significant changes in attitude. Doctors need to give the public a broad and favorable perception of themselves and their services.

Historically, the restraints on advertising imposed by medical societies were instituted to protect the public from unrealistic—and sometimes even false—claims by members. They guaranteed the public would not be subjected to advertising that might erode public confidence in the entire profession.

Now the public, through its governmental institutions, has decided that freedom of speech is essential to an informed public, and that restrictions that interfere with that process are unacceptable.

These circumstances pose a new challenge to the medical profession: to evolve methods of expanding its channels of communication with the public without transgressing reasonable ethical guidelines—methods that will enable the public to obtain responsible information and at the same time preserve public respect for the profession's dignity and standards of conduct.

While the debate has been focused on advertising, the problem of how best to proceed has been explored through other techniques by numerous pioneers in medical service marketing. It has been evident to them for a good many years that the use of public relations methods is more acceptable and more dignified than advertising.

Compare the relative merits of, for example, a half-page *advertisement* about a particular medical specialty with a half-page *article* in the same location in the same publication discussing the exact same subject matter. The article has greater credibility. Because it appears as part of the publication's editorial matter, it bears the stamp of approval of the publisher and the editorial staff.

Despite the fact that such efforts sometimes raise eyebrows in medical circles and prompt discussion of ethical guidelines, the trend has been growing steadily for several years. This has happened because the public is hungry for medical information. Very hungry. There has been a genuine explosion of interest in health issues and fitness. And medical knowledge is an essential ingredient of that interest.

In response to this growing public appetite, all the media have expanded their coverage of medical and health facts and developments. A host of new health-oriented publications has appeared. A great many publications as well as radio and TV stations have added medical experts to their staffs to insure responsible scientific comment and news coverage.

Today's intensified coverage of health issues has created an opportunity that far-sighted medical people have learned to utilize effectively. They have made it their professional responsibility to engage in communication processes that provide the public with reliable, comprehensible, up-to-date information.

Public relations offers a variety of opportunities to engage in this process. Examples abound: Guest appearances on discussion shows on radio and television. "How-to" books on medical subjects written by doctors. Guest editorials on health, or health-related, topics of public interest. Articles either authored by or quoting a doctor acquainting the public with his or her opinions, experience, and insights. Syndicated health and fitness columns that appear in numerous publications. Plus more narrowly focused opportunities such as participation in local meetings where health, fitness, and related issues may be part of the agenda.

On the one hand, each of these activities provides a needed public service. On the other, each represents a dynamic and powerful way of increasing public awareness of the specific doctor and his or her expertise. The availability of such opportunities is having a profound influence on how professionals can built their practices. Compared with these uses of the media, hanging-out-a-shingle-and-listing-oneself-in-the-Yellow Pages lacks impact. And waiting for word-of-mouth referrals takes many years.

Several years ago, shortly before the first Supreme Court decision on the subject, a few doctors and other health-care professionals began approaching me to obtain professional public relations guidance. I recognized that our efforts could set new precedents regarding what is acceptable and responsible.

My firm had previous experience with medical associations, hospitals, clinics, and pharmaceutical companies. We had already devised policies for these organizations designed to   1. inform the public,   2. market specific specialized skills, services, and products, and   3. meet high standards regarding responsible, dignified, professional behavior. We had prepared spokespersons, arranged appearances, placed relevant articles, all scrupulously within ethical guidelines.

It seemed to us that whether we represent an organization or institution, such as a hospital, or an individual, such as a doctor, was a far less significant issue than whether the presentations that result provide the public with accurate and practical information in a tasteful, ethical manner.

We decided to take the plunge. We began by representing a Midwest plastic surgeon and a New York area dermatologist. Our approach consisted of several elements aimed at informing the public and at presenting the doctors in a manner that would generate deserved public confidence. They both became so well known that, despite professional pressures to curtail their appearances and other "marketing" activities, they succeeded in carving out unique positions for themselves.

As a result of our success with them, my firm was sought after by other medical professionals. Soon, in addition to the original clients, we represented specialists in the fields of opthalmology, orthopedics, podiatry, psychiatry, and gastroenterology. We set up a section of the agency to work exclusively in medical public relations and established a set of operational guidelines. The guidelines enable us to help professionals market themselves ethically. We not only avoid efforts that might jeopardize their reputations—or those of their fellow specialists—but we also work to bring honor, recognition, and credit both to them and to their colleagues.

Our guidelines include the following: We begin with in-depth staff interviews with the client. We probe, searching out the elements that individualize our clients. We look for their personal contributions to their field of practice. We explore how their uniqueness relates to their specialization. Until this process occurs, our clients are often unaware of their own achievements and distinctiveness. We pursue this process by interviewing other professionals in the field, attending seminars, and even sitting in on patient consultations.

We then explore how awareness of our clients' skills and unique attributes can benefit the public. We examine the degree of public interest in their field and the receptivity of the media to various potential article ideas, interview concepts, and show-segment suggestions.

Next we devise a program aimed at establishing the client as a spokesperson for his or her field. The program usually addresses all types of media. Depending on the client's specific needs, it may encompass national media or it may tend to concentrate on local media. But each portion of the campaign is part of an overall, focused effort.

The possible vehicles are many. We may stimulate a publication to do a round-up article that quotes the client extensively. We may place articles carrying the client's byline that discuss material of interest to the public. We may arrange interviews with writers, reporters, or syndicated columnists. We may arrange for interviews on radio or TV talk shows.

The public is seldom aware of these public relations efforts. They take place behind the scenes. To the public it appears that the media quote the doctor simply because he or she is well known or is a recognized expert. Most often it isn't that simple.

The process avoids the potential opprobrium associated with direct advertising. There is no risk of public rejection or professional censure. We also work with the doctors on how to speak to the media—that is, how to translate complicated medical terminology into language the media and the public can understand. We help them become comfortable with camera and microphone. We work with them on how to handle delicate issues and tricky questions. We help them to understand how to make the work of media people easier while advancing their objectives and at the same time contributing to the reporter's understanding of medical facts. All this helps the client become an effective spokesperson for his or her specialty as well as an effective marketer of personal services.

Over the years, many medical professionals have undertaken to use public relations techniques on their own. And, in fact, many have been successful. But public relations is not their specialty. Physicians seldom know how to approach the media. They aren't aware that editors and producers are wary of people who don't know how to present their ideas in media terms. They are also wary of self-promoters. The doctor may call the wrong person, call at the wrong time of day, offer the wrong kind of article, pose ideas in language that is too technical for the media person to understand, or may be too self-serving to generate genuine interest.

Public relations professionals know how to approach the media and how to help the doctor set the right tone. A doctor who seeks professional public relations help can rightly expect the following:

• Public relations can get a name before the public, achieving enhanced name recognition quickly and associating that name with a specific set of skills.

• Unless the doctor has done something sensational it is unrealistic to expect the public to know what he or she has achieved. But being the subject of, say, a segment on *Good Morning, America* will bring the doctor's viewpoint, outlook, expertise, and manner into public awareness in an emphatic way.

• The doctor should expect a campaign that is balanced between national and regional or local exposure.

• The campaign should be systematic, not hit-or-miss. It should have a timetable, a written plan, a set of article themes, interviews, and targeted media.

• The doctor should expect a campaign to have identified objectives. And they should be well-suited to the doctor's marketing needs.

- The doctor should realize that it takes about two months for a public relations program to begin to generate identifiable results. After the initial interview, it takes time for agency people to become oriented to the doctor's specific area of expertise, prepare background materials, develop well-thought-out and relevant queries, prepare the client for appearances, and work ideas about his or her expertise into media schedules.

- In this context, doctors should generally look for and expect reports of some results within three months. And written reports on progress and contacts made on the doctor's behalf every month.

- Throughout the relationship, the doctor should expect ongoing interaction with the agency. It may be necessary to discuss alternative article ideas, have photo sessions, sit in on strategy meetings, or for the public relations staff to develop deeper familiarity with his or her activities in other ways.

A doctor who employs public relations professionals who work in this way can expect to become much better known and to be sought after by people who are in need of the precise medical services he or she provides. And the entire marketing effort can be accomplished in an ethical, dignified, professional manner.

Results for medical practitioners can be remarkable. One doctor we work with is now a regular medical commentator for a Los Angeles news show. Another has a nationally syndicated column. And one plastic surgeon had a television feature film made about one of his more dramatic case studies.

What this means for doctors is more patients, more income, and wider recognition of their achievements.

We work not only for individual physicians but for the medical profession. We were hired by the Medical Society of the State of New York to promote a public image for it that would help stave off or at least mitigate hostile legislation designed to encourage malpractice suits. We followed this up by approaching a number of individual specialists, some of whom were very nervous about being the first in their profession to use public relations. One of our earliest clients was a Midwest physician engaged in a highly exciting state-of-the-art practice in plastic surgery. We went to the media with this story; our client began to be widely mentioned and his practice tripled within the first year of his hiring us.

Another client is a New Jersey dentist who had developed a technique for making dentures at a single sitting, saving his patients hundreds of dollars. We placed stories on him telling about patients who came into his office with diseased teeth and went home that same day with a complete set of brand new dentures. We described how he was setting up a system of franchised dentistry offices in Manhattan, Westchester County, and New Jersey. Almost overnight, the dentist became a celebrity and an ironical thing happened. He became so wealthy that when he got involved in a divorce suit with his wife the court added half a million dollars to the settlement price on the worth of our client's name alone, which by this time had become known from coast to coast.

Our efforts with doctors and dentists have attracted widespread attention. We have turned several of them into the authors of best-selling books, and gotten them and others on television shows, enabling their incomes to skyrocket.

We developed a marketing concept for one plastic surgeon based on the premise that people don't realize what they really look like as various moods take hold of them during the course of a day. They may glance in the mirror in the morning and evening—that's it. Our plastic surgeon client has set up a center where people can receive a total physiognomy review with a clinical psychologist doing the interviewing. The patient sits before a camera. While she's engaged in conversation, the psychologist evaluates the video tape. He will point out to the sitter that her nose looks bigger when she smiles. She creates wrinkles in her forehead when she becomes stern or angry and so forth. The psychologist trains the patient to become aware of the facial changes induced by her various moods and to control them as far as possible.

This approach has triggered a great deal of interest. We have written a host of feature stories, firing the imagination of erstwhile jaded magazine editors who are only too eager for a new angle. This is what creative public relations is all about.

Purists may be upset at the idea of the medical profession using public relations to get its message across to the American people. Yet PR, like any other business tool, can be used for public benefit as well as harm. It all depends on the integrity of the user and the public relations practitioner. In generating publicity for plastic surgeons, we have increased their income, true, but we have also helped, for instance, to educate women about the various new types of mastectomy available. We have helped inform women who face drastic mastectomy surgery that reconstructive and cosmetic surgery can help them lead more normal lives.

In representing the American Optometric Association, we have helped educate millions on how to care for their eyes; how to choose contact lenses; when to wear and when not to wear them. We have spread the message that men too can improve their appearance and help their business careers by availing themselves of advances in cosmetic surgery; and that cosmetic surgery for men need no longer be kept secret. We've made the public aware of new drugs, new surgical procedures, new technology offered by hospitals and clinics.

I have always been fascinated by the challenge of applying PR to new uses. Recently the Federal Trade Commission ruled that professional associations may advertise and make use of PR to build their practices.

As a result, we were hired by the world's largest accounting firm, Coopers & Lybrand, to generate publicity for them. Nowadays there's virtually no organization that isn't eager to place its story in the media through public relations. This includes even major religious denominations.

One of the last bastions of professional conservatism was the legal profession. Lawyers have been among the last people to consider using publicity to attract clients. Indeed, lawyers have traditionally told their own clients to say "No comment" to questions by news reporters and were no more ready to be accessible to the press than they advised their clients to be. However, under the stimulus of new federal trade regulations, and pressed by increasingly tough competition, law firms have begun to discover the advantages that public relations can provide. We are in the forefront in representing them.

Prestigious law firms are not willing to advertise openly. They prefer to get their message across in a more subtle way through public relations. A prominent law firm will engage a public relations organization to discreetly place news about it in the media.

Readers today are being confronted with an increasing number of newspaper stories in which attorneys express opinions on a wide variety of issues. As certain lawyers are quoted time and again as authorities in real estate, corporate, or criminal law, the news reader develops an awareness of their expertise. The typical law firm that comes to us has an area of business it wants to expand—for example real estate, finance, or trust and estate litigation. A financial writer gets an assignment from his editor to write on, let us say, the future of real estate. We are able to direct this writer to a lawyer in one of our client law firms and obtain an opinion for him on real estate law. Being used for attribution as a source of background information is a chief means of publicity for a law firm. We make our lawyers readily available to the press and have not been surprised to find that our lawyers love giving advice; it's what they're accustomed to doing anyway.

<u>CHAPTER TWELVE</u>

PUBLIC RELATIONS: THE UNIVERSAL SKILL

Whether we realize it or not we all use public relations. When we try to advance our interests by persuading others, we succeed or fail to the extent that—unknown to ourselves—we are able to adapt PR principles to our own ends. Public relations is not some arcane and sophisticated discipline, used only by a group of "image makers" who work for entertainers, politicians, and big corporations. It's a tool that can and *must* be used by anyone determined to develop his or her full potential in any area involving human relations. PR has become so pervasive that it's hard to imagine a field or activity where it cannot be or is not usefully employed. One may be a veterinarian, an architect, a lawyer, the head of a local Four-H Club, a high school football coach or PTA president. Anybody who needs to relate to the public in order to sell himself or herself—or his or her services or skills—has to get a message across.

Everybody recognizes how important it is to get mentioned in a newspaper article or book. The reverence even the most sophisticated people have for the printed word is extraordinary. The fact that someone appears in print is enough to convince the public that this individual has something authoritative to say, that he or she is somebody.

One of the more common misconceptions about personal PR is that it is simply a matter of getting attention, and that therefore the best strategy is to think up the most spectacular stunt. People dream up the zaniest stunts to get attention. Not long ago I read of an acrobat who announced at a press conference he was going to walk across the continent on his hands. He figured it would take him 10 years to accomplish this feat, at the end of which he would have a dramatic book to write that would certainly make the best-seller lists. While he could be in for a rude awakening, it is true that anybody with the ambition and the desire can become his or her own promoter. It is impossible to be a physician unless you are trained in medicine. It is not possible to be a lawyer unless you are trained in law and court procedures. There are also highly trained and experienced professionals in the PR field, but average persons can adapt PR principles for themselves, using common sense and applying the methods that we discuss in this book. Anyone can pick up the phone, call a newspaper editor, and if he has something of interest, find a receptive ear.

But because there has been increasing competition to get into the news, it is necessary to create news "happenings." Something is happening almost every day that properly presented is news copy. All that is necessary is that the individual recognize when something is newsworthy about him and his experiences.

If one is looking for a job that is being sought after by a dozen other applicants, one of the best things he can do in advance is to write an article for a publication in the field he's applying for. For example, if he is an accountant looking for a job at an accounting firm his chances would be enhanced enormously if he could get an op-ed piece into his daily newspaper on, let us say, why accounting regulations should be made stricter.

Most daily newspapers carry many op-ed articles. They are not all written by people who have academic or professional credentials. Some are written by ordinary citizens. Someone writes about the need to clean up the downtown area of his city; another, about ways to cut down on muggings or fires. If anyone applying for a job can show, along with his resume, evidence that he is publishable, he is of particular interest to an employer.

Anybody can also generate news. Almost anybody with average skills can learn how to write a press release that will attract the attention of even the busiest editor. It doesn't matter who we are or where we live; we all have something to offer the local newspaper or television station. If you're a member of a garden club and wish to announce that you are having a meeting next week with a guest speaker, all you have to do is pick up the phone and call the local editor. You can phone the information operator to find out the number of the *St. Louis Post Dispatch* or the *Westport News* or the local radio or television station. Anybody can ask for the news desk and somebody will answer the phone to listen to what you have to say.

This nation is hungry for information and almost all of us have acquired some kind of specialized information by virtue of the kind of lives we lead. A great deal of this information is of value to other people and anyone who is prepared to share valuable information can get the necessary publicity.

Many people do not realize that they are doing extraordinary things, the news of which can bring benefit and hope to others. They perform spectacular feats, yet fail to see the tremendous value of what they're doing. But often it takes a PR person, trained to detect merit in everyday jobs, to bring out the true value of what is being done.

This is particularly true of medical research people—the physicians, chemists, biologists, and technicians who frequently perform miracles in their work in hospitals, universities and pharmaceutical companies. To them it's likely to be just part of the job. For example, several of us were interviewing a research chemist for a pharmaceutical firm. We knew he was involved in an important project, but it seemed impossible to get this truly humble and dedicated man to see it that way. For half an hour he talked about retorts, test tubes, how chemicals are blended, and so on, often in jargon that was virtually impenetrable.

Finally I said, "Dr. Smith, forgive me for interrupting, but I have just one question. Can you tell me, in a few words, the sum and substance of what this will do?"

He blinked at us, then said mildly, "I guess what I'm trying to say is that this will save millions of lives when it comes out."

I wish that good people everywhere would master the basics of public relations, not necessarily to promote themselves or their causes, but simply to be able to see, from the public point of view, the interest and real worth in things that they consider ordinary.

The following pages cover the principles of good public relations. They are basic, to the profession and to the lay practitioner as well. While you may not decide on PR as a career, I think you will find basic ideas you can adapt as you build your own strategy to achieve your own goals.

CHAPTER THIRTEEN

THE PRINCIPLES OF GOOD PUBLIC RELATIONS

In *Confessions of an Advertising Man*, written more than 20 years ago, David Ogilvy described the principles of good advertising. By now, dear reader, you are familiar with the essential differences between advertising and public relations. Advertising buys space in newspapers and magazines and time on radio and television and proceeds to persuade you that brand X is better than brand Y. Public relations does much the same thing except that generally it works within the side of print media and the news and talk shows of radio and television which, in this country, cannot be bought.

Yet the essential goal of both advertising and public relations is essentially the same—to persuade people to do something. My clients, like those of advertising agencies, hire my firm because they too want their target audiences to do something: buy a product or a service. And the service can range from choosing the right doctor to buying the right soft drinks.

When I address groups of new employees at my agency, I make it clear that we will be tolerant of many types of personality traits and characteristics, but that no one can work at our agency who does not abide by our eleven principles of sound public relations practice. Many will sound obvious, but it has been our experience that they need to be addressed and abided by.

1. Tell the truth.

There's no question that public relations plays an advocacy role, just as law and advertising do. We work on one particular side of an issue. Even marketing a consumer product is in essence an issue. If you represent a tea, then the other side of the issue is coffee or other brands of tea. If you're selling a Democratic candidate for office, in essence you're opposing Republicans.

What is unique about the democratic form of government in the United States is that it allows the expression of all opinions on all subjects. One can advocate or oppose capital punishment; champion a Communist candidate or a mainstream one; support the PLO as well as the State of Israel; encourage the expansion of wilderness areas or the intensification of urbanization; take up meditation or aerobics—and so on and so on.

The media are bombarded by public relations representatives advocating all manner of issues, causes, products, and services. Ultimately, whoever presents the most compelling case tends to get the ear of the media. This is where the power and professionalism of public relations come in. We in public relations are essentially advocates who present our cases for our clients before the jury of public opinion.

While it is true that one can create a number of points of view based on the same set of facts, the facts must be accurate. The media rely heavily on public relations practitioners to present accurate facts and information to support arguments. There are far too many issues in contemporary society for the media to have the wherewithal to check all facts and information completely. They must often rely on public relations professionals to do this and if we let them down, the media will let us know it.

In my organization anyone who distorts facts and information to the media will be dismissed.

2. Be persuasive.

What does this mean to a public relations professional? It means essentially the same thing as it does to the legal profession—the ability to present facts in a manner that leads to the desired conclusion. Just as a trial lawyer must be able to marshal all of his facts and powers of persuasiveness before a jury to plead his client's case, so must the public relations profession plead its case to the jury of public opinion through the media.

How does a public relations person learn to be persuasive? Through a variety of means. The ability to write clearly and powerfully is a common denominator among public relations professionals.

The ability to communicate on one's feet is also extremely important. Public relations professionals must also be able to convince and persuade clients and companies that the approach they are advocating is a sound one. Once the client is convinced, the next step is to communicate with the media. The most effective professionals in the public relations field are those who are able to persuade writers, reporters, editors, and broadcast producers that the story idea they are advocating is right for the particular media. To accomplish this, a public relations professional must be quick of mind and convincing in a one-on-one meeting.

Can this be taught? Not entirely, I believe. Since a public relations professional must also be an effective salesman, all of those traits that are normally associated with a good sales-

man—or a good lawyer—are important to the public relations profession as well.

3. Believe in your mission.

If I am being entertained by a member of my firm at his or

her home, I expect that person to serve our clients' products. For example, since we have been representing Schweppes for some time now, I would expect that if I asked for a mixed drink that included tonic water, I would be served Schweppes.

By the same token I will not represent any product, cause, or situation that is alien to my personal belief system. For example, I would not allow our agency to represent countries like Libya or Syria. Nor would I represent the Ku Klux Klan or any group that espouses violence as a means of creating solutions. In this sense public relations is different from the legal profession. Many lawyers are called upon to be public defenders when those indicted do not have the means to pay for their own lawyers. There is no equivalent mechanism in the public relations field. If legislation were ever introduced making it incumbent upon the public relations field to represent organizations without visible means of support who advocate unworthy causes, I would personally rally the public relations profession to oppose it.

4. Be imaginative.

Aside from advertising and the entertainment field, I don't believe there is any other single profession that offers as many opportunities to be as resourceful, daring, outrageous, and imaginative as public relations. The function of public relations has expanded to the point where it is involved with virtually every facet of contemporary American life.

Since the ultimate goal of public relations is to persuade and influence, there is almost no limit to the means used to achieve these goals. Public relations presents an opportunity to career-minded individuals to expand their horizons, depart from journeyman and traditional techniques, and come up with ideas that have never been tried before. How many professions can boast of this?

For every mile a swimmer was able to swim around Manhattan island in a recent campaign, the Leukemia Society was able to raise thousands of dollars in contributions. As it turned out the swimmer exceeded the world's record for distance swimming for a woman. What better way to achieve both publicity and public awareness of the need to combat leukemia?

Eagle Rare Bourbon developed a program that was consistent with its name to preserve and rehabilitate the American bald eagle.

Hertz Rent-A-Car developed a program to honor the outstanding high school athletic performances by a boy or a girl in each of the 50 states.

The examples are just too numerous to itemize in a single book. It would amaze you to discover the countless feats of imagination and resourcefulness that have been applied by companies, associations, government, and the public sector to persuade and influence the public. Let's just say that the public relations profession casts its eyes on talented and resourceful individuals who recognize that in order to persuade and influence, they must put their imaginations to work in ways that would rarely be needed in other professions.

5. Be Prepared.

Use your imagination also to anticipate everything that could go wrong—and forestall it. As sophistication and technology make everything more complicated, this skill becomes more important.

Technology is a blessing that one can turn into a curse. Today it is possible to produce incredibly intricate audio/visual presentations. They can be very impressive—when they work. But, when they don't work, it can be disastrous.

Let me take you to the Grand Ballroom of a posh Reno hotel. The room is filled with more than 1,000 franchisees (and their families) of a national real estate franchise operation. This is the all-important annual sales meeting, during which the franchisees must be motivated and inspired.

I was observing this event because we had handled the PR for the company. The gathering was about to witness a spectacular multi-media presentation put on by the franchise company's advertising agency.

Huge sums had been spent by the advertising agency in mounting this presentation. It involved dozens of screens, projectors, audio systems, television monitors, film, slides— all coordinated by a computer. At the rehearsal it had been dazzling.

The meeting started. The president of the franchise company spoke for a couple of minutes. Then the multi-media show came on. For five minutes it wowed the audience. Then, suddenly, the screens blurred and went dark, the sound trailed off and stopped. The crowd was patient—at first. These things happen. We waited . . . and waited . . . and waited . . .

But the show never resumed. The computer could not be restarted. The ad agency people, shattered, slunk from the room. That afternoon they were fired.

It was the most embarrassing fiasco I have ever seen. But witnessing this calamity taught me something. I determined I would resist with all my strength getting into a situation where I would have to rely completely on complicated forces outside my control.

In other words—Keep It Simple!

6. Do your job as though your life depended on it.

Does this sound strong? Not to me. I have always lived by the principle that there is no problem that cannot be solved. And further, there is no person that cannot be reached. There is no red tape that cannot be untangled. And there is no bureaucracy that cannot be penetrated.

I am continually amazed at how people will take just so many steps toward solving a problem and proceed no further, being satisfied that there is no solution. The same people often wonder why their mind-sets do not enable them to proceed further in their careers.

There are countless examples of how individuals have been able to overcome seemingly insurmountable odds when either their lives or the lives of their loved ones depended on it. If your loved one were in an accident and was in a hospital bed crying out for you, wouldn't you tear down walls in order to get to that hospital as soon as possible? Would you be deterred by the fact that the battery in your car didn't work, or that it was a cold and wintry night, or that the buses were no longer running? If you had to get to that hospital, your flow of adrenalin would somehow get you there—and in plenty of time.

This is the way it should be in the world of business as well. When people in my firm exceed their norm and carry out their functions as though their lives depended on it, then success will always be achieved.

7. Be a good listener.

This is an overused but underheeded injunction. Most of us are not effective listeners.

My firm has obtained a great deal of new business during the past 10 years. We have as clients some of the most respected and well-known organizations in the country. I personally believe that one of the reasons we are effective at converting new business prospects is because we have paid attention to listening to people.

Clients enjoy describing their organizations, their concerns and considerations, their marketing goals, their industry, and their plans. Whenever I go into a new business meeting and meet an individual for the first time, I make certain that, for the entire duration of our meeting, he or she is doing the bulk of the talking. When someone begins our discussion by wanting to know more about my organization, I turn the tables immediately by saying, "I will have ample time to describe my organization to you, but I'm more interested in what your organization is all about. Could you give me some background on your goals?" This usually appeals to most individuals, who would rather do the talking. I have been in many situations where I've barely said a word throughout an entire discussion because I have made it a point to allow that individual to be expansive. Many times I've gotten feedback that I seem to be on the same wavelength as that individual and appear to be competent and professional. Why? Because I wanted that individual to let me know about himself and his goals.

The art of listening applies to more than just using good common sense and allowing somebody to explain his needs. It is also crucial because the more information you have, the better your recommendations will be. You cannot help or understand a client or a sales prospect by briefing him about yourself before you've had a chance to learn about him—and making recommendations before you know enough about the prospect's business or organization.

While this may seem to be simple common sense, I can assure you that listening is an art that is not practiced by most people.

8. Unless you're a good juggler, find another field.

While it is true that within the public relations field there are many areas of specialization, the good generalist will forge ahead and do well professionally. I personally believe a top public relations agency executive can achieve distinction in any field that requires outstanding management capabilities. Public relations executives like George Weissman of Philip Morris have gone on to become heads of Fortune 500 companies.

Being an account executive in a public relations firm is probably one of the most difficult jobs in the world, but at the same time one of the most rewarding psychologically. A typical public relations account executive in an agency must be able to work on a number of activities at the same time. A public relations professional generally must be able to juggle assignments, accommodate crises and emergencies, and meet strict deadlines. The public relations professional must be a counselor, a fine speaker, an excellent writer, a resourceful, imaginative person and must be tactful, diplomatic, persevering, and productive.

The challenges are great but the personal rewards are also great. While tedium and boredom have no place in the flow of events in public relations life, job burnout is a distinct possibility. Public relations is a "what have you done for me lately?" profession, and the battery has to be constantly recharged.

Thus if you're contemplating public relations as a career, know in advance that you must be a disciplined, well-organized person able to handle a number of things at the same time. If you're already in the public relations field, know that you can forge ahead professionally by demonstrating you can manage your time well and can roll with the daily punches.

9. Walk Tall.

The public relations field today has no need for sycophants. It needs bright, strong-willed, assertive individuals to walk tall, speak their minds, and carry out programs that contribute to the good of the client or organization. All others, seek another profession.

My business partner, Amelia Lobsenz, personally spearheaded a movement under the auspices of the Public Relations Society of America to educate the public on what the public relations profession is. It was called "PR for PR." This was a novel approach for the profession to take, because while public relations represented every other activity in contemporary American life, it had still not been able to communicate its own story of the growth of the profession and its present-day role. Lobsenz met with editors and writers to bring them up to date on the practice of public relations today and the people it attracts. As a result of her efforts, many publications that had traditionally been uncomplimentary about the public relations field began to take a fresh look at it. One of Lobsenz' goals was to point out to the media that the two fields need each other and should respect each other. The fact the media subsequently began to report more and more favorably on the public relations field was a tribute to her endeavors.

Once the media would never consider covering the public relations field itself. Through efforts like those of Amelia Lobsenz, the media are beginning to look at their half-brothers, public relations professionals, in a new light. The media are beginning to understand that public relations is a respectable calling and, like any other, merits media coverage of developments within the profession itself.

Bill Moyers, the television journalist and commentator, did an hour-long special on historic leaders in the public relations field. He called attention to the work that the great Ivy Lee did for the Rockefeller family and how Edward L. Bernays helped to commemorate the anniversary of the discovery of electricity by Thomas Edison.

Bernays, who is still going strong in his nineties, was interviewed by Moyers. He described how the public relations profession has grown through the years. It was a shining moment for those of us in the public relations profession.

10. Be outrageous.

Here we need a definition of terms. Outrageous can be defined as intolerable or violent in action or temper. This is not the definition I'm referring to.

The definition I prefer has to do with being bold, daring, resourceful, and imaginative—and taking risks. Public relations has no place for individuals who always play it safe. Since public relations is based to a large extent on the development of creative concepts, I am often amused at the results of the internal brainstorming sessions during which our professional people attempt to develop creative ideas for clients. There are some who are satisfied with traditional, "safe" ideas. The ones that I follow with great interest are those who take the shackles off and go for broke. These are the people who will be truly outrageous—and in the process will come up with brilliant ideas that ultimately take shape and substance— and work.

Inherent in the process of being outrageous is the ability to look at life—as well as clients—with a twinkle in one's eye and a sense of humor. Brainstorming sessions at our company have some very specific and clear guidelines. No matter what idea is brought up, the rules assure that the idea will not be disparaged or attacked no matter how outrageous it is.

We look for outrageousness. We do not discourage it. Therefore, in response to an idea that is thrown out before the group, it is forbidden for anyone to say "that's crazy. That idea will never work. It's just not practical."

When we brainstorm, we are not looking for finished details or execution. We like to start with the germ of an idea and it doesn't matter what shape it's in when it comes out of an individual's mind.

When our firm was one of three finalists for the New York Marriott Marquis Hotel account, we dispatched our troops to the conference room and began our traditional brainstorming. We were trying to come up with ideas for the opening ceremonies of the brand new luxury hotel when somebody jumped up from her seat and shouted "I've got it." With eager but wary eyes focused on her, she said. "You know how when they unveil a painting or a statue there's usually a curtain or veil over them. Why can't we do the same thing for the Marriott Marquis? About two weeks before the hotel's grand opening, let's put the largest veil ever created over the entire hotel. When it's time to unveil the new structure, we will have a hundred helicopters lift the veil up and away to reveal to the people of New York City and the world the sleek elegance of this new luxury hotel."

Despite the fact that her idea was truly outrageous—on an outrageous scale of one to 10 it ranked a full 10—it was greeted with excitement by the other members of the group. During our representation to the Marriott management, we actually included this idea along with artistic renderings of our suggestion. Although the idea was not subsequently used by the Marriott people, my firm did get the account. What got us the business was our willingness to stick our neck out and be different.

Being different doesn't necessarily mean being better, but combining being different with a well-thought-out plan of execution often makes a great difference to companies in how they view their public relations strategists. If an outrageous idea is to be implemented, it obviously must be well thought out and the practicality of the idea looked at carefully.

Here's an example of being outrageous. When I speak before management and public relations groups, I am usually asked to supply a biographical sketch. One day my secretary suggested that it was time to update the sketch I had been using for such purposes. As I sat down at my trusty typewriter to redo this major document, I felt a mood growing within me that reminded me of what it must have been like for Dr. Jeykll to change into Mr. Hyde. Suddenly I was transformed from a serious businessman into a whimsical, outrageous rebel. Instead of writing a traditional biographical sketch of myself, I wrote the following:

Ever since he was named public relations director of P.S. 92 at the age of five, Art Stevens has contributed substantially to the disparagement of the public relations field.

His definitive treatise "Public Relations Among the Dinosaurs," published in the prestigious *Harvard Animal Review*, continues to be widely quoted and has earned for him the enduring professional respect of present-day dinosaurs and their families.

His first business venture, a lemonade stand on Mapes Avenue, became so successful that it was acquired by General Foods. Aggressively utilizing the cash generated from the acquisition, Mr. Stevens purchased six raincoats, making his successful foray into his next profession—flashing—immediately successful.

During the years that followed, Mr. Stevens could be seen on IRT subway cars in New York practicing his profession to the delight of hundreds of thousands of New Yorkers. Mr. Stevens holds the voyeurism record of achievement for having peered into 7,421 separate windows. For this achievement, he received the coveted "Big Eyes" Award conferred annually by the American Optometric Association for creative users of the eyes.

Listed in *Who's Who in the Bronx*, Mr. Stevens, his wife, and two monkeys reside at Attica Prison.

I sent this "revised" biographical sketch to some of the managers in my firm and asked them if they had any suggestions on how to improve it. With the same seriousness with which I sent my biographical sketch to them, the managers to whom it was sent circulated it back to me with such comments as "it reads well, but it's too self-serving." "I think you may be too modest. Wasn't it actually 12,000 windows you looked into?" "Isn't *Who's Who in the Bronx* the briefest book ever published?"

As you can see, whimsy was met by whimsy. I not only encourage outrageousness among serious-minded public relations professionals, I nurture it.

11. Crave knowledge.

Or, to put it another way, if you think you know everything there is to know, then you're in the wrong field.

The most rewarding part of public relations, particularly from the agency point of view, is the limitless number of new fields you tend to become immersed in. Since the goal of public relations is to inform and persuade, this goal cannot be accomplished without absolute and total knowledge of your subject matter. Again, I'd liken this total fascination with knowledge to the work required by a trial attorney to prepare his case. The trial attorney, with the help of his staff, pores over every law book, every statute, every precedent-establishing case, all levels of testimony, and more. When the good trial attorney thinks he has his case ready he wonders what vital pieces of information from the puzzle he may have neglected. The more prepared the trial attorney is, the more airtight his case becomes.

So it is with public relations. The more curious and knowledge-hungry an individual is, the more effectively he will represent his client or company. Nowhere is the accumulation of pertinent facts and information more necessary than during the process of presentations before prospective new clients. Among the reasons always given to a loser in a new business competition is that the firm didn't bother to do its homework. The firm was interested in talking about itself rather than taking a good hard look at the prospective client's problems and challenges.

The firm that usually gets the business is the one that has poured a good part of its efforts into research and fact-finding. If we are presenting before a consumer product company, before we even have our first meeting we make certain our people have used the product, spent hours at stores in which the product is sold, and had discussions with store owners, users, sales representatives, and distributors. We scour the media for past articles about the product and its competition, we do perception studies among the media to determine how the client and the company are perceived, and we review success stories by other public relations firms for similar products. And when we have our very first meeting with a prospect, we make certain we know as much as we can about that prospect so we can begin to ask penetrating and intelligent questions. We have to assume that we are meeting with a client because he believes our credentials are appropriate for him. Thus we spend less time on presenting our credentials than we do on absorbing knowledge about the client.

Since a great deal of what we do involves representing a client's story to the media, we have to try to be several steps ahead of the media and anticipate their comments and questions when we present article ideas to them. Thus our office very often takes on the look of a city editor's desk in a major newspaper. Our professionals are out backgrounding their news stories so they have enough answers for the media to present our clients' cases as effectively as we can.

In addition to immersing ourselves in our clients' subjects, we want our people to be naturally curious about the world at large as well. We look for "whiz kids" who know a little about a lot of subjects. We like our people to be just as comfortable discussing the previous day's baseball scores as they are discussing the current opera at the Met. We want people to be interested in the arts, the humanities, psychology, politics, world events, and esoterica in general. In public relations all knowledge will eventually be put to good use for a client's cause. I urge public relations professionals everywhere to spend countless hours playing the game Trivial Pursuit.

CHAPTER FOURTEEN

How to Make Your Business Grow: Without Hiring A PR Firm

Businesses that make or sell products are likely to build a public relations program around their products—endorsements, unusual applications, and so on.

With the rapid growth of the service side of the economy in recent years, there has been a corresponding surge in the quest for ways to promote firms that deal in intangibles. In addition to working with many product-making companies, we have made something of a specialty of developing PR strategies for service companies.

The marketing of services has become much more sophisticated in recent years. One of the reasons for this is that many professionals, once prevented from engaging in competitive business solicitations, are now much freer to promote themselves. At one point members of medical societies, accounting associations, and bar associations were restrained from openly soliciting new business because it was considered unethical and unprofessional. Those days are gone. Today you see lawyers, doctors, accountants, and many other professionals vying for attention by advertising, engaging in public relations, and taking whatever marketing steps they need to attract attention and generate new business.

If you're a beautician in Idaho, a lawyer in Florida, a plastic surgeon in Colorado or a plumber in Los Angeles, you can benefit from new business techniques that are generating business for some of your own competitors in the marketplace. These techniques can be used without hiring a public relations or an advertising agency. By using these techniques it's possible to increase your business with a minimum of expenditure.

1. Find a way to be different from your competitors.

If you're a lawyer with a general practice, determine which area of your practice you excel at the most and carve out a niche in it.

For example, you might want to focus on tax law, divorce law, estate planning, or writing wills.

If you're an orthopedist, you might want to focus on sports medicine. If you're a beautician, you might want to specialize in skin-care for mature women. And if you're a plastic surgeon, you might want to convey that you're in the forefront of new surgical techniques for tucking and hiding.

2. Coin your own terms.

There's nothing that seems to convey greater expertise to the public than being identified with a particular word or slogan that you've invented.

In an article I once wrote for *Harvard Business Review* I coined the term "brandstanding" to reflect the use of special events in marketing. This term came to be identified with me. It attracted considerable attention and began to be used almost generically to describe the phenomenon that the term was created to explain. I made certain that credit would go to me each time the term was used by other professionals. The fact that it was coined in a highly regarded business publication did me no harm.

While head of Ted Bates Advertising, the late Rosser Reeves coined the phrase "unique selling proposition" to reflect what he assessed to be the correct advertising approach. Reese and Capiello, another advertising agency, rode on the coattails of a term they invented which also described how advertising can best be created to sell products—"positioning."

The coining of terms is perhaps best used by politicians running for office. William Safire has caught the flavor of American politics through the definition of its many terms and slogans in his political dictionaries. Be the first on your block to follow his example.

3. Take one of your successes and milk it for all it's worth.

In the public relations field, one of my competitors, Richard Weiner, had the good fortune of being associated with the Cabbage Patch Kids. His firm was the agency of record when the Cabbage Patch dolls burst on the American scene and were snapped up at record speed. As a result of the manner in which the Cabbage Patch dolls caught on and the tremendous amount of publicity they were given, Weiner's name and his firm have often been associated with one of the great American marketing success stories; this despite the fact that Coleco, the parent company of the Cabbage Patch dolls, was in such financial difficulty as a result of its other businesses that it had to end its relationship with the Weiner firm. Another case of winning the battle and losing the war. However, Weiner took advantage of the celebrity status accorded the Cabbage Patch doll and used that case study to market his firm aggressively. I tip my hat to a capable and savvy colleague.

In advertising, Doyle, Dane, Bernbach became associated early on with the tremendous success of the Volkswagen advertising campaign.

F. Lee Bailey, the celebrated attorney, had a string of early successes as a trial lawyer defending notorious defendants. As a result his later career, though less widely covered by the media, remained highly celebrated.

Sit back and think about what you regard as the most successful episode you've ever been involved in; one that shows the service you provide to greatest advantage. Once you've focused on this, then proceed to the next series of activities.

4. Write ten articles a year in your name.

This is such an obvious way to achieve visibility for you and your service—and your successes—that I am truly surprised that so few people consider this option. I do it myself and it works wonders.

Pick out 10 publications that reach your target audiences. Included in the list should be daily newspapers in your area, consumer magazines, and trade publications. If you feel you're not an accomplished writer, here's a way of doing it that might make it easier for you. Choose your subject first and make sure it makes reference to what you feel is one of your greatest achievements or successes. Then be prepared to give advice. If you're in a service business, surely you have accumulated enough wisdom and experience to offer your customers or clients advice. If you're a plumber, surely you can advise your customer on how to keep his pipes from freezing in the winter. If you're a beautician, you can offer your customers advice on how to keep skin from drying when traveling from one climate to another. And if you're a tax lawyer, surely you must have some tips on how to outwit Uncle Sam.

Buy an audio cassette recorder, sit back one evening after downing your evening cocktail, and talk to the recorder as if that recorder were one of your customers. Give that recorder some good solid advice as only you can. Just start with your basic premise—"how to keep your pipes from freezing"—and go from there. Pour into the cassette recorder everything you feel your customer needs to know based on your experience.

Arrange to have the cassette tape transcribed by a local secretarial service and take a good hard look at what you have set forth. Not only will you have sown the seeds for one article, you probably will discover that you have others to offer. Write a letter to the editor of all of the publications you'd like to have your article appear in. Tell these editors the subject of the article, what advice you would like to pass along to the readers of that publication, and why you're qualified to write the article. I can assure you that your suggestion for an article will fall on responsive ears.

5. Use direct mail to generate business.

Direct mail is a service business that also happens to be one of the fastest-growing in the United States. You can buy almost anything by mail these days, as the number of mail order catalogs you receive will attest. You too can use the techniques of the direct mail professional to generate business.

All you need to do to get new business inquiries through the use of direct mail is to write a good letter and send it to a good list. If you live in a small community, your best list is probably the telephone directory. If you live in a large city, you can buy lists of target customers rather inexpensively. A direct mail list can cost you as little as $25 for a list of 1,000 names.

The next ingredient is the writing of an effective letter that convinces a prospect you can accomplish a great deal for him. Despite the fact that you might be writing to hundreds of people, each letter must be personalized. Each target person must be made to feel you are writing specifically to him or her. Remember, a letter that begins with "Dear Sir or Madam" or "To Whom It May Concern" will generally wind up in the garbage can. But a letter addressed to "Dear Mrs. Jones" will most likely be read. It is flattering to a prospective customer that he or she has been picked out by you as someone who could benefit from your services. If the timing is right, you will get your fair share of inquiries and telephone calls.

6. Bring your possible customers all together.

Or putting it another way, run a clinic, a seminar, a symposium, or a private breakfast.

Let me cite a few examples of what I mean. My firm runs a coffee and Danish breakfast once every two months for our clients and our guests. This informal get-together usually includes about 100 people. Quite an array of subject areas are covered during the course of these breakfasts. Their real purpose is to create top-of-mind awareness on the part of our clients and our guests that we are doing something exciting and worthwhile. It is not intended to be a hard-sell setting, but simply a place where important public personalities can share their views with our guests.

Recently we co-sponsored a two-day seminar for marketing directors, product managers, advertising directors, and public relations directors on the subject of Special Events in Marketing. I acted as moderator and also gave the keynote address. This seminar was on a paid attendance basis, and attracted close to 200 attendees from throughout the country. We had selected a "hot" subject, and the attendance and the resulting awareness of our role in this field were of great value to us professionally.

No matter what business you're in or service you provide, you too can avail yourself of the opportunity to bring groups of people together. You can bring a group of your target customers together to hear you personally render advice on your field of expertise or you can run an inexpensive coffee and Danish breakfast similar to the one I just described and invite a personality from the community to speak. Or you can bring two or three people together to form a panel discussion that you can moderate on a subject connected with your expertise.

These programs can be covered by local media so that you can obtain extra mileage from them. They can be held in local hotel facilities, or a private room at a restaurant, or a meeting facility in a school. If you shop around you will find you can obtain more than adequate facilities at a reasonable cost.

I suggest you run these programs as a series as opposed to only one. If the first several are successful and the programs are sufficiently interesting, then you will have no problem getting attendance at future programs. The invitations can be in the form of a letter that is individually typed on a word processing machine to reach your target lists.

7. Get to know the media in your community.

Do not be awed by the media. Reporters, writers, editors, and producers are human beings like the rest of us. They too put their pants—or pantyhose—on one leg at a time. Make the media aware that you have expertise in your field and can be a resource for them to draw upon. Very often a reporter will be working on a roundup article that requires quotations for attribution to a number of different sources. There's no reason why you should not be quoted in an article giving tax tips to the public during income tax time if you're a lawyer or accountant; or energy-saving tips if you're an engineer or a plumber; or skin-care tips if you're a physician or dermatologist.

The best way to acquaint the media with your credentials is to call and ask for an appointment. Step one in this process is to make sure you know the names of media people and what their areas of responsibility are. If you're a lawyer, you might want to get acquainted with the business editor of your daily newspaper. If you're a beautician, then the women's page editor is for you. If you're a sports doctor, the sports editor is the one you will want to chat with. Do your homework first, get a list of the appropriate media people, and go to work.

Conduct a survey and publicize it. Surveys in the form of percentages and statistics are always of great interest to the media. An example of this is the attention given to political polls around election time. Conduct an informal study among your customers. If you're an estate lawyer, send a written questionnaire to your clients and find out such things as how many of them have wills, how many of them are leaving the bulk of their estates to one individual, and other questions that might come to mind on this particular subject.

If you're a physician, you might want to do a survey of your patients' preventive medicine practices. If you're a beautician, you might want to do a survey of beauty habits.

You might need the assistance of a market research professional who can help you frame the questions, tabulate the responses when they come in, and show you how to develop the conclusions. You should write up the survey's conclusions and offer them on an exclusive basis to one of the newspapers in your area. At the same time, you should prepare a mailing that summarizes the survey's conclusions to be sent to your customers and your target customers. Surveys reflect knowledge and expertise and invariably will lead to new business inquiries.

If you follow these rules, your service business will continue to grow and will help fuel the nation's economy. Trust me, they work.

CHAPTER FIFTEEN

GETTING INTO THE PAPERS AND MAGAZINES

Newspapers need news. (So do radio and TV news shows.) Your business or community interest needs publicity. You and the newsmedia can work to each other's mutual benefit—if you understand what news is—and if you're able to package it in usable form.

Are you the publicity chairman of your garden club or civic group? Are you on the welcoming board for a social event? Is there an opportunity to give a luncheon honoring a leader in your community? Can you invite your local assemblyman or war hero to address your organization's monthly meeting? Can you hold a talent contest giving awards to the kids in your community? Can you run a show for your neighborhood's pets? Can you connect your activities to a service-oriented theme? Newspapers, magazine editors, and television producers are eager for news.

Although editors always welcome newsworthy developments, you must learn when and how to approach them. If you think you have news, by all means call the editor. But at the same time you must learn to understand the psychology of editors—how they react, when they react, why they react.

When I started out during my Prentice-Hall days, I began by visiting editors who I decided were meaningful to my company. Whether one is public relations counsel for a corporation or is working for oneself, the technique is the same. You must target the editors and the media outlets most likely to respond to what you have to offer. At Prentice-Hall my immediate goal was to reach the community in which we operated. I wanted to convey that Prentice-Hall cared about its community. Next I was determined to acquaint the book publishing industry with what the company was doing. Also, I was anxious to reach shareholders and prospective shareholders since Prentice-Hall was an American Stock Exchange company. Other goals were authors we hoped to add to our list and readers for the books that Prentice-Hall published.

After I made up my list, I proceeded to call each important editor and try to establish a personal relationship. I learned at the outset that there were pitfalls in approaching editors; in fact I stumbled into one almost immediately. The first editor I decided to introduce myself to was the business editor of the *Bergen Evening Record*, the daily newspaper in the community where we had our corporate headquarters. After some trepidation, since I had never dealt with an editor before, I determined to take the bull by the horns. I picked up the phone and began, "My name is Art Stevens, I'm the public relations director of Prentice-Hall. I'm calling to say hello." There was a moment of silence. Then a voice at the other end of the phone responded abruptly, "Okay, hello!" And hung up. I was stunned. Later I found out I had made a classic mistake. I had called the editor when he was racing to meet a deadline.

My late afternoon call was a decided "no-no" in dealing with a daily newspaper. All professional public relations people know this. Those who are not professionals must learn to understand that deadlines have to be respected if one is going to deal with editors. I would have been much better off calling this editor at ten in the morning when he was planning his day, rather than phoning him at four in the afternoon when the copy boy was standing at his desk waiting for copy to rush to the printers.

Your first step in dealing with the media is to learn the ground rules. Once I understood this and started phoning editors at a time they could talk to me, I was able to get beyond "hello."

Once you get to know an editor you must *establish your credibility* with him. The most important thing to an editor, whether you are a professional public relations person or the president of a civic group, is belief in your integrity, so that if he goes out on a limb for you he knows that you have furnished him with accurate information, that you are not blue-skying anything, that you are giving correct quotes and so forth—in short, that you are not using him to promote something that turns out to be hot air. Once that happens that editor will never deal with you again. If, however, an editor is able to rely on you as a credible source of information, you will forever have his ear.

The usual way of contacting an editor is through a press release. You put down on paper a description of the event you are involved with and would like the newspaper to carry. It could be anything from the speaker you have chosen for your next bingo club meeting to the fact that the local museum will have a special exhibit of Japanese art beginning next month and there will be a public reception the first night. This is news to your local community and you obviously want people to know about it.

How do you write an effective release? Every editor receives scores of releases and has time to read through only a small number of them. An editor working on a deadline has to determine very quickly what is of genuine news interest and what can be disregarded. Most news releases are ignored for a variety of reasons. The news value has not been made clear, or the release has been written in such a dull manner it is of no interest to an editor. Those news releases that stand the greatest chance of being accepted are ones written in a crisp, journalistic style.

If you pick up your newspaper you will notice that news stories are written according to a formula: the most important element of the news being reported appears in the first paragraph and each succeeding paragraph presents facts in order of their decreasing importance. This is so the newspaper reader, if pressed for time, can, by scanning the first paragraph of a news story, receive all the vital information he needs. Let's assume that a fire has broken out in Macy's department store in New York. Here would be a professionally written first paragraph. "A fire broke out in Macy's 34th Street yesterday afternoon, killing 40 people and injuring 10 others." If you read nothing beyond this you would know essentially what happened. The second paragraph might go on to say, "The fire, which started in electrical wiring on the fourth floor, began discharging sparks at noon but firemen were not alerted until an hour later when smoke filled the entire store."

Writing a press release is different from orally recounting news to a friend. If you had been at the scene of the Macy's fire you would probably say afterward, "Joe, something happened today that you won't believe. I was walking down the street and all of a sudden I smelled smoke. I got closer. I saw fire engines all over the place and someone said, 'Gee, there's a fire in Macy's.'" You presented this news to Joe in narrative form, building up to a climax. But when you are writing a news story it can't be done that way. You must present the essentials immediately and as briefly as possible. Many editors, particularly on smaller newspapers, don't have time to do their own writing. If a release is written in the same style of reportage the newspaper uses, the chances of getting it published are increased. The editor will just pick up the release and use it as is. Obviously, if you want to place a news release in your newspaper, it pays to study its style as carefully as possible.

In preparing your release, write the date on which you want the news to be published. Underneath this write a short headline summarizing, in a few words, the information contained in your release. Your headline should allow the editor to grasp at a glance what your news report is about, permitting him to make a fast judgment as to whether it's worth further study or should be tossed in the wastebasket.

Here's a lead that conveys the relevant facts concisely and with impact.

SINGER INTRODUCES
THE EASY MENDERS
CLOTHING CARE APPLIANCES

(*NEW YORK, June 24*)—*The Clothing Care Operations unit of The Singer Company, North American Sewing Products Division, today announced its entry into the small appliance field with The Easy Menders*—four unique, portable, clothing care appliances for repairing seams, hems, holes and tears and for reattaching buttons.*

Each subsequent paragraph should contain additional facts in order of their declining significance. You should compose your press release in such a way that the editor can extract whatever he needs from your press handout and fit it easily to his requirements. He may have to cut your two-page release down to three paragraphs to meet his space needs. If you have done your job properly he will know the gist of your story immediately. Be sure you have attributed any factual claim you make to somebody whose name is given. Your release must provide the authority for all your facts and statements. You should mail your release so that it is on the editor's desk no later than the day before the date of the release. If you want to see your story appear in the Friday morning newspaper, you should drop it in the mailbox no later than Wednesday afternoon, if it is marked for local delivery.

Here are the remaining paragraphs of the release whose lead we quoted a moment ago:

"The Singer Company recognized the need for quick mending ap-

pliances for busy people with little time, and for those men and women who normally dread attempting even minor clothing repairs," said Stephen J. Kind, president of the division. "These products are the first easy-to-use, quality mending appliances on the market."

The new line includes:

- Tiny Taylor* mending machine, an easy-to-use, lightweight, pre-set mending appliance for a variety of apparel mending and alteration needs; powerful enough to stitch through several layers of fabric;

- Match-A-Patch* hole and tear mender, a simple-to-use, hand-held repairing appliance which makes durable and nearly invisible patches to hide holes, tears and cigarette burns;

- Button Magic* button sewer, a hand-held device which reattaches buttons with thread in less than two minutes; and

- Stitch-Me-Quick* hem and seam tacker used for emergency repairs on hems and seams as well as non-clothing repairs.

"These are state-of-the-art mending products which fit in perfectly with today's busy lifestyles, saving both time and money. They can be used at home, in the office or when traveling. The Easy Menders are a complete family of mending appliances designed to help everyone cope with life's little rips, tears, holes and missing buttons," Mr. Kind said.

National distribution to the consumer begins this summer, and The Easy Menders clothing care appliances will be sold by the newly organized clothing care operations unit chiefly through the houseware departments of major department stores via manufacturers' sales representatives.

"We have created a new appliance category," said Robert P. Soutter, director of marketing and sales for this product line. "We have a high quality, inexpensive, easy-to-use line of products which appeal to everyone—regardless of sex. Their ease of use makes The Easy Menders suitable even for teenagers. The agony of losing a button or ripping a garment knows no demographic boundaries.

"Virtually every type of clothing mending need is covered by one of the four Easy Menders," Mr. Soutter said.

Match-A-Patch hole and tear mender

This sophisticated hole, tear and cigarette burn mender makes virtually invisible, professional patches which can withstand repeated washings and cleanings. Match-A-Patch hole and tear mender works on almost all fabrics, including wool, cotton and synthetics, and will not scorch.

Button Magic button sewer

Unlike other button stitching appliances which use staples or plastic, Button-Magic button sewer attaches buttons with real thread. This simple, hand-held device can replace 2, 3, and 4-hole buttons in less than two minutes through the simple squeezing and releasing of the machine lever. It is perfect for use in the office or when traveling.

Stitch-Me-Quick hem and seam tacker

Stitch-Me-Quick hem and seam tacker is a lightweight, hand-held appliance used for on-the-spot repairs of hems and seams on pants, skirts or coat linings.

Stitch-Me-Quick hem and seam tacker works on all fabrics and, because it is so portable, it can also be used around the house for jobs such as tacking curtain hems.

Tiny Tailor mending machine

A mini-tailor shop, the Tiny Tailor mending machine is lightweight and portable (weighing less than six pounds) and is perfect for mending seams, patching and minor alterations. It was not designed for clothes construction. Tiny Tailor mending machine comes pre-set without the need for any tension or pressure adjustments by the user. It can stitch *through several layers of material (including up to six layers of denim), and can be easily threaded for fast color changes.*

# # #

*A Trademark of The Singer Company

Here's another example of the press release.

"PLAYTEX CHALLENGE" OFFERS MILLION DOLLAR PRIZE TO WOMAN TENNIS PRO WHO CAN WIN ON FOUR SURFACES

(NEW YORK, August 31)—*One million dollars, the largest single prize in the history of any sport, was offered today by Playtex to the professional woman tennis player who can win four major tournaments on four different court surfaces in the course of a tournament year.*

Called The Playtex Challenge, this award for the first time places women ahead of men in terms of monetary rewards.

The announcement was made by Walter Bregman, Chief Executive Officer of International Playtex, Inc., at a luncheon at the Essex House.

"This will at last elevate women's tennis to the financial dignity it deserves," said Mr. Bregman. "Through the years women's tennis has struggled to reach parity with the men's game. Now it is ahead, and Playtex, a company long identified with women, is proud to initiate this significant breakthrough.

"The key feature of The Playtex Challenge," noted Mr. Bregman, "is that it links the women's tour in an exciting, cohesive way. At last there will be no question as to who is the consummate woman pro. Victory in top-flight competition on four challenging surfaces will prove who is the Queen of women's tennis."

The action was warmly applauded by the Women's Tennis Association, many of whose members attended the press conference.

"We welcome the Playtex Challenge enthusiastically," said Billie Jean King, the retiring WTA President. "It's an innovative concept that will lend a strong undercurrent of excitement to the pro tour. This is one challenge we're happy to accept."

Dr. Julie Anthony, clinical psychologist and herself a former tennis pro, has been named the Director of The Playtex Challenge. In this capacity, Dr. Anthony will serve as consultant and spokesperson at the four major tournaments and throughout the year. She will represent The Playtex Challenge to the press and the tennis community.

The four tournaments comprising The Playtex Challenge start with the U.S. Women's Indoor Championship at Minneapolis September 28-October 4, to be played on carpet turf; move to the Family Circle Cup at Hilton Head, S.C., held April 5-11 on clay; then to the 1982 Wimbledon championships next June 21-July 3 on grass; and reach a climax in the 1982 United States Open at Flushing Meadows August 31 through September 12 on hard court composition.

"To win the $1,000,000 the same player must win all four tournaments," said Mr. Bregman "If she wins three of the four she will receive $500,000."

Playtex, which celebrates its 50th anniversary in 1982, is a leading manufacturer of women's apparel and feminine hygiene and beauty products, and is a wholly owned subsidiary of Esmark, Inc., a large publicly held, multifaceted company.

This year Chris Evert Lloyd won the Family Circle Cup at Hilton Head on clay and Wimbledon on grass, and goes into the U.S. Open as the defending title holder on a hard surface. Tracy Austin won the 1980 U.S. Indoor title on carpet and the Family Circle Cup on clay in the same year.

Three championships, however, are needed to take $500,000 and four to win the entire award.

"Playtex is delighted to be able to offer this prime incentive to women's tennis," said Mr. Bregman. *"Over the years, Chris Evert and Martina Navratilova have each won more than $2,000,000 and young Tracy Austin last year passed the $1,000,000 mark, but now it will be possible for a woman of championship caliber to win one million in a single year.*

"The competition is going to be fierce. It may very well serve to bring back veterans such as Billie Jean King into the crucible of regular competition. It will certainly inspire the youngsters to even greater heights."

A hand-crafted sterling trophy will be presented to the winner.

# # #

The press release is the most common means of conveying news to an editor. But as you develop your contacts and get to know your editor better, the nature of your activities may lend itself to a more ambitious news form—the feature story. If there is reason for a newspaper or magazine to do a feature article about your activities, don't send a simple news release. The press release is connected with events; the feature story is about people and the human interest angles relating to them. Since a feature article is not primarily concerned with presenting news facts it will not follow the structure of the news release but will lend itself to a variety of treatments depending on the nature of your subject.

Here's a feature story that whets the reader's interest and conveys a lot of information.

GOOD-BYE TO THE "FOUR-EYES" WEDDING BELL BLUES

Do you wish you didn't have to walk down the aisle wearing glasses? Has your doctor ruled out soft and hard contact lenses? Was it due to a specific vision problem that the soft lenses could not correct—and are hard lenses too uncomfortable for you to wear?

Perhaps now is the time to ask your doctor about a new type of contact lens, called the rigid gas permeable contact lens. This lens is the fastest-growing kind of contact lens. It is virtually as comfortable as a soft lens, corrects many vision problems and offers the visual clarity of traditional hard lenses.

Why the need for rigid gas permeable contact lenses? The first contact lenses, standard hard lenses, were developed in the 1950s and are made of tough, inflexible acrylic plastic. Hard lenses are versatile for correcting most vision problems and have the longest life span of all contact lenses. However, they can occasionally fall out of the wearer's eye, especially during vigorous activities, and hard lens wearers often experience "spectacle blur"—poor vision when switching from lenses to glasses—due to oxygen deprivation of the cornea, which needs to "breathe." Hard lens wearers also have been known to complain of discomfort after many hours of wear.

By contrast, rigid gas permeable contact lenses are made of flexible plastics that allow oxygen to reach the cornea. It is expected that they will eventually replace conventional hard lenses, which will soon become virtually obsolete. By 1986, estimates are that the number of fittings for rigid gas permeables will climb to 26 percent, and hard lenses will drop to 3 percent of fittings for new contact lens wearers.

The rigid gas permeable lenses offer many advantages to the contact lens wearer. Unlike hard lenses, they require no "break-in" period, and don't burn, tear, make one sensitive to light or cause spectacle blur. They are easier to care for than soft lenses and help correct high degrees of astigmatism that soft lenses do not. The state-of-the-art among the rigid gas permeable lenses is The Boston Lens® II Contact Lens, which has the highest degree of oxygen permeability. The Boston Lens® is the only contact lens that has a conditioning and cleaner solutions system developed especially for it.

Soft lenses are made of various flexible water-absorbing plastics, making them oxygen-permeable. They are popular because they are often more comfortable at first than hard lenses, and are difficult to dislodge, even during sports. However, they must be replaced more often and require more complex daily care with expensive solutions than hard lenses, and cannot usually be worn by people with extreme astigmatism. Soft lenses are now available in tints that can change eye color, even from brown to blue, which may make them appealing even to people who require no vision correction. The Boston Lens® is available in a blue tint, not to change the color of the wearer's eyes, but to make it easier to see if dropped.

Extended-wear soft lenses are among the newest developments in contact lenses, and can be worn continuously up to two weeks. The water content of the lenses is very high, allowing a great deal of oxygen to reach the eye. Users of extended-wear lenses must return to their eyecare practitioner three or four times a year for checkups and cleaning, and the lenses are less durable than other types of lenses.

Now that you are armed with the facts about contact lenses, why not visit your eye doctor to see if the rigid gas permeable contact lens can meet your vision needs? If so, you'll have one less worry on your wedding day: your glasses won't slide down your nose when you kiss the groom.

# # #

Frequently, once you have suggested an idea for a feature story to the editor he will want to have the actual story written by a member of his staff. Usually at this point in your relationship, you will be welcome to drop by and discuss the idea with the editor informally, but it is always better to bring him a written outline of the story you are suggesting. Often it is desirable to submit photos along with the idea for your feature story. Since the story deals with a human interest angle connected with people, it will be enhanced by pictures of them.

In conditioning yourself to think about public relations lines, ask yourself before you prepare a news release or feature story suggestion, "What is my angle, my slant?" Try to be trendy, try to connect your news to current events, and above all, remember you must tailor your releases to the needs of the publication you've sent them to.

The calendar provides clues for angles. Holidays are staple foundations for feature stories. Here is the lead from one such feature:

MAKING HOLIDAY CLOTHING GIFTS LAST

Clothing is a favorite holiday gift. But remember that beautiful pink blouse your husband gave you last Christmas? Your best friend accidentally burned a cigarette hole in the sleeve; here comes another Christmas and that new blouse just hangs in your closet, unrepaired.

This Christmas make sure those expensive presents of clothing you give—and receive—survive for many holiday seasons to come.

If you have a business story and wish to get publicity for it you will find a greater receptivity today than ever. With a rising number of Americans becoming investors and a growing interest in business and financial information, these stories have advanced in recent years from the back to the front pages of the American press. Once, dry facts and statistics comprised the bulk of business news reporting. Today the spotlight has shifted to business people in the news and the field is becoming increasingly personalized and humanized. The emphasis is on stories and pictures about people in addition to the usual economic charts.

If you have an informative, interesting business story to tell, you will find it easier in many respects to place with an editor in a business paper than it would be to place a general news story in the daily newspaper. A business editor is not compelled to select news that will interest the mass public. Business editors are interested in reaching specialized fields. (This is especially true of trade magazines.) And if your story has information for even a small market, the publication addressing the readership of that market will be most receptive to you.

The amount of space devoted to business in the daily newspaper is considerably less than that devoted to general news, so the competition for space can be more vigorous. The typical business section in a daily newspaper, apart from the stock tables, consists of two or so pages.

If you are involved in an enterprise in which there are public investors and you have bad financial news, don't try to hide it. Be forthright in announcing the adverse news as soon as possible, because it is going to be found out anyway and your credibility is the most important asset you have with editors. The best strategy is to make a clean breast of the bad news quickly—let it be known from the start. If the bad news is leaked out in dribs and drabs the stock will go down each time a morsel of the news is handed out, but if you let it all out at once so that it can be discounted at the start, once the worst is known the stock will in many cases rebound smartly.

You don't have to be a professional public relations practitioner to get publicity in the media. If you can offer an editor something that is newsworthy or that provides information that will be of particular interest to his readers, you can gain his attention. As life becomes increasingly more complicated, people who can provide valuable information are playing a pivotal role.

Many editors who are swamped with work are only too eager for outsiders to do research and information gathering for them providing that what is put into their hands is accurate. This is especially true on the smaller daily newspapers. Once newspapers essentially covered on-the-spot news—for instance, reporting that a fire broke out, or a crime occurred in a downtown supermarket. But in recent years more and more space is devoted to information pertaining to the lifestyle of readers, sociological surveys, medical and health reports. These are subjects that can be handled expertly by public relations firms. It's therefore not surprising that as more and more newspaper space is given over to such articles, editors are placing increasing reliance on material supplied not by staff reporters, but by public relations people.

The small dailies often urgently need outside help. On publications with tight budgets, the editor-in-chief sometimes doubles as the religion editor, the sports editor, and the real estate editor, when he is not out covering weddings. If someone sends in public relations-generated material that provides useful information or an interesting human interest story, more often than not the editor is going to pick it up. The editor may call the PR person to get background color and have some of the story filled out in greater depth, and perhaps follow this up with some interviewing by his own staffers to expand the story, but essentially he will use what the public relations person sent in.

At one point I taught public relations at Fairleigh Dickinson University. I would have each student in my class pick five news articles at random from the daily press and bring them into class, where we would discuss the probable origin of each news story. Upon analyzing the material we would find that a substantial proportion had the earmarks of being public relations-generated.

A significant percentage of the news stories in even the august *New York Times* are public relations-inspired. That does not mean that every article originates from a public relations firm and has simply been dressed up by the reporter. Many political articles originate from the President's press secretary in the White House or from other Washington agencies. Even though these don't come from commercial PR agencies, they are nevertheless PR-originated. What holds true for the *New York Times* also pertains to the *Wall Street Journal*. Not long ago, while testifying in court, public relations consultant Edward Gottlieb demonstrated that a large number of financial and business articles appearing in the *Journal* originated in PR firms representing corporate clients. In other words, the notion the average person has that what he reads in the newspapers comes entirely from the typewriters of the editors and reporters is only partially correct.

While the press is open to the legitimate placing of public relations material, if you want to place a message, you cannot hope to hit your target by firing buckshot. You must draw a bead and hit a specific bull's eye. You cannot send out the same story to a number of different newspapers; you will only wind up offending the editors. Each publication differs in its need; each has its own type of readership, its own demographic base, its own way of handling stories. Unless you have studied a publication and learned thoroughly about its requirements you have no business sitting down with its editor to discuss story ideas. Never call your daily newspaper unless you know exactly what an editor likes to write about and how he presents his articles.

Amelia Lobsenz started out as a freelance writer for magazines. When she went into public relations she concentrated on placing publicity with magazines. She worked closely for a number of years with John Mack Carter, editor of *Ladies Home Journal*, and then with Lenore Hershey, his successor. Once, while running a seminar at New York University, Amelia invited Lenore and John to be her guests on a panel discussion. Carter by this time had left the *Journal* and had gone over to *Good Housekeeping* and Ms. Hershey had taken over his old job. Just before the seminar session began, Ms. Hershey entered the room with a shopping bag that she handed over to Carter. "John, here's a present for you. These are letters addressed to you." "But Lenore," John replied, "why should people send letters to me when I have not been editor of *Ladies Home Journal* for nine months now?" "I know," Lenore observed, "this shows how up-to-date some PR people are."

This anecdote illustrates that even some public relations professionals do not study the magazine to which they are sending material carefully enough. Anyone who had examined the *Journal*'s masthead would not have written a letter to an editor who had gone on to another publication nine months earlier.

Each publication has its own requirements. If the big city daily is not interested in your civic association meeting, the local shopper or the local weekly might be. If the press in your community reports only the news on a city and state level, try to make your subject, local though it may be in origin, part of a bigger feature, if you can. If not, look around for a publication that does report on your kind of activity.

Editors have become more sophisticated in their requirements. Today magazines know in greater detail than ever who and what their markets are. They have to know this because Madison Avenue advertising agencies cannot possibly sell advertising to their magazine clients if they do not provide them with this specific kind of detailed demographic information. However, while magazine editors are much more demanding in the precision of the material they require, there are many more publications to approach today than 10 years ago, even though the magazine industry has lost some big publications. Now that we have become a highly diversified society there are publications for all interests and tastes: physical fitness, antiques, health and beauty, fishing, sports cars, stamp collecting, and so forth.

Because of this diversity and specialization, anyone who wishes to place a story in a magazine should read at least six back issues carefully before contacting the editor. See who is writing what; learn what the story angles are. Study the magazine's competition so that when you phone an editor to follow up on your press release or go in to visit him, you will be able to suggest ideas that are absolutely on target.

Remember, editors are not ogres. They are as anxious to run an interesting, informative article as you are to place it with them. However, it is important for you to understand the psychology of an editor in a responsible position on a publication. To be successful, he must exercise excellent judgment. The best editors are the most thoughtful ones who display a genuine empathy with their readers. The editor of a consumer magazine aimed at families who live on farms or low-income people in city apartments cannot afford to look down his nose at someone who is trying to run a household on $12,000 a year. If the editor really feels the problems of his readers in his gut, he will do a good job for his magazine. The qualities that define a successful editor are the ones that also define a successful public relations person.

Bear in mind, when you are preparing to approach an editor, that the most marketable ideas are service-oriented, "how-to" articles. If you feel your subject is a mundane one of only minimal interest to readers, give your imagination a chance to play around with it. There are few subjects so humdrum that they cannot be dressed up to make an exciting human interest story. There is virtually nothing so unimportant that it cannot be given significance with the application of creativity.

Let us assume that you are trying to get publicity for a client who makes paper clips. To try to place publicity on clips per se is probably futile. However, it is entirely possible to take this subject and develop it into a feature that will whet an editor's appetite. Don't view the article as something simply about paper clips. Place the paper clips in the context of a larger theme; for example, an examination of the role of paper clips in the office of today; or information on how the paper clip has changed historically over the years. Since the most effective angle in placing the story is the service one, you might relate the paper clip to a service-oriented problem. Another way of presenting this story is to create news around it. For example, you might do a survey on current new uses of paper clips. (Surveys are very popular with editors.) Perhaps you can hitch the story of paper clips to the profile of an interesting personality. Stories about people usually generate more excitement than stories about things. Perhaps you can do a survey to select the office manager who has found the most imaginative use for paper clips. You might suggest to an editor that he run a contest to give an award to the Office Manager of the Year. In short, you have transformed a story about paper clips into an exciting human interest feature to entice magazine readers.

To summarize, study your target publication carefully. Go over the masthead listing the names of the editors and staff writers. In some cases it is suitable to send your release to the editor-in-chief; in other cases the associate editor or a staff writer should be your quarry. In still other cases, you should send it to a columnist who writes regularly for the publication. Needing to fill his space every month or week, as the case may be, with lively material, the columnist is always on the lookout for material from any source. In still other instances, you might be better off finding someone who is a specialist on the subject you are promoting and whose articles appear regularly in the publication. If you are dealing with a health topic, for instance, find out who is the writer specializing in health articles. (The names and addresses of these writers can be found in the *American Society of Journalists and Authors* and other similar directories.)

It is true that many editors are ambivalent in their feelings about public relations people. On the one hand, they are wary because PR people represent a special interest. On the other hand, editors need reputable, reliable PR practitioners because when an editor is pursuing a story, he needs background information, facts, statistics and so forth to document the interpretation he is giving the story, and frequently the public relations person is the best source of material that is absolutely essential for the completion of a story. To save money, publishers have been cutting their staffs, making it even more opportune for reputable public relations people to serve as sources for them.

Years ago many stiff-necked newspaper editors had strong

reservations about taking any material at all from public relations practitioners, but there is far less of this today. Journalism schools now teach courses in public relations. Ed Gottlieb relates that several years ago the dean of the New York University School of Journalism informed him that he was against the idea of having public relations taught at NYU, but bowing to the demand of students, he hired a public relations professional for his teaching staff. Subsequently, the dean completely changed his attitude. Today he is not only eager to have public relations taught as part of the curriculum but he has a professor on his staff who was formerly the head of a PR agency.

Edward L. Bernays, at 93, is one of the giants of the public relations field. Through his doctrine of "the engineering of public consent," he has been a major contributor to the persuasion explosion.

CHAPTER SIXTEEN

GETTING YOUR MESSAGE ON RADIO AND TV

You need not confine the advocacy of your cause to print. If you know the ropes you can use radio and television as well.

I frequently tune in to local radio stations in various parts of the country while on business travel. While listening to them I have heard an assortment of guests—the local veterinarian explaining how to care for pets, the head of a local museum discussing exhibits that are scheduled in the coming weeks, an officer of the local Planned Parenthood Association describing various family planning methods. Frequently these representatives of causes, associations, and businesses initiate the contact with the stations themselves. They call and say, "I'd love to be a guest on your show. I'm a veterinarian and I think people would be interested in knowing how to care for their dogs in the summer heat." It's easier to be on radio and television than most people realize and yet, like in everything else, a strategy must be devised.

Gabe Pressman is an expert on how TV and radio people select the news they carry. A pioneer in television journalism, Pressman has been on the airwaves since the early days of the medium. He is a virtuoso at asking the penetrating question and has interviewed everybody from U.S. Presidents and foreign leaders to New York City mayors and civil rights leaders.

I asked Pressman how much of a chance an average citizen, wanting to publicize himself or a cause or a business he is involved with, has of getting the attention of the television news desk. Pressman answered by citing his own experience. Between 4:00 and 6:00 p.m. daily, while he is ensconced in one of the NBC rooms writing his script for his evening news show, his telephone rings every five minutes with someone at the other end declaring he has a "big story" to tell. In order to ward off this barrage of seekers for TV publicity, Gabe confesses, "I disguise my voice and I say, 'Pressman is not here now. Call back after six or six-thirty.' Some public relations executives get very ruffled by this response because they prefer to be on their way home at that hour. Unfortunately, I also get rid of some nice people in the process."

Pressman is eager not to turn away the outsider who has a meritorious story to tell. The important thing is that it be the truth, not a hoked-up bit of razzle-dazzle designed simply to get a plug on the airwaves. "My grandfather," says Pressman, "stressed one word to me when I was a kid—*emess*. I don't know very much Yiddish, but the word *emess* means the truth. There's nothing like the truth; it's the greatest public relations tool in the world. If you can convince a reporter something is true and he is a strongly committed journalist, he will fight for you."

Given the extraordinary competition to get on the airwaves, what can the average person do to gain attention for his debating club in Great Neck? "Write a note that's very pointed and succinct," advises Pressman. "State the issue and why you think it deserves publicity and why a wider audience than your friends will be interested." While the same techniques can be used over the telephone, unless your story is an urgent one that has to be placed within hours, Pressman suggests you write a letter instead. For the individual who has successfully sold the TV news desk and won a place on the airwaves, Pressman has further advice. When the average man or woman manages to get on TV and the camera is turned in their direction, Gabe is asked a common question. "Do I look at you or do I look at the camera when you are interviewing me?" And he answers, "Look at me because it's more natural that way. If you are looking into the camera you appear to be spaced-out. The anchorman for the evening news show may look with impunity into the camera but not the interviewee."

The reason for not peering into the camera, Pressman adds, is that it ordinarily makes the person look bad since television is an artificial medium. The camera is also merciless in detecting the con game artist. If the interviewee is being factual, honest, trying no gimmicks or phony gestures, the camera will convey the truth of what he has to say and the integrity of the person he is.

Pressman observes that there are amateurs, with no training whatever, who are intuitively talented public relations people. Indeed, some are masters at using the tools of the trade. Pressman points to the mayor of New York City, Edward Koch. One of Koch's gimmicks, which almost never works for anybody else, is that he breaks the rules and looks directly into the camera when he speaks. During a TV interview, Koch answers a few questions, then he turns to talk directly to the people "out there" as if he were saying to the news reporter, "The hell with you—you're only a reporter." He's like a lawyer addressing a jury—ignoring the judge and everyone else in the courtroom and looking right into the jury's eyes.

As for the chances of an unknown individual getting his story on television, there are a lot of people who have a real or fancied grievance, Pressman points out. Perhaps one person out of 15 offers a legitimately newsworthy story. How does Pressman judge who is worthy of TV exposure? "I look upon myself as a surrogate for the public, and I judge on the basis of what I feel the public wants. I am an upper-middle-class

guy and I obviously cannot, except in my imagination, understand people in the ghetto or the guy in Queens with a bottle
of beer watching a football game, but at least I try. I try and
imagine what concerns them. I am a man, not a woman, yet
I believe in reporting as much as possible on matters that
concern women."

One of the reasons TV news editors are wary of people trying
to snatch publicity on the airwaves for themselves is that there
are organizations specializing in street demonstrations and terrorism primarily for the purpose of getting on television. The
staging of street demonstrations for television became a finely
crafted strategy in the 1960s. People would set up picket lines
and phone to alert the news desk. "The television and news
desk people had no sophistication in those days," Pressman
observes. "They would cover every picket line reported to
them." Now there is an increase in selectivity by the news
desk. It is much more wary, more choosy, less likely to be
taken in.

Nevertheless, street demonstrations for "social causes" continue to represent a high-powered weapon of public opinion
moulders. Pressman notes that a number of nonprofessional
people have an uncanny instinct for PR. "They're community
activists and they work the streets. They know all the news
desks and the networks and they even know who to call on
the desk at each TV station to announce that a demonstration
will take place."

For people who are not self-trained activists but who desire
to get publicity for less dramatic endeavors, one of the factors
that has eased access to radio and television is that under the
regulations of the Federal Communications Commission, all
broadcasters by law must allocate part of their airtime free to
public service activities. If you have a message to get across,
the fact that it lacks commercial or news value to a network
may not hinder its acceptance of it. Members of every community in which the broadcasters operate must be heard and
allowed to air their concerns. This is not the case with newspapers or magazines.

Moreover, to have to continually think up programs that will satisfy viewers is not easy for broadcasters, TV writers, or talk show hosts. Television devours such monstrous quantities of script material that broadcasters are constantly on the lookout for new ideas. They can be very receptive to what you have to offer if it promises to attract viewers.

To approach a TV or radio station, use the basic strategy used in preparing a news release, but in this case, instead of sending it to an editor, submit it to the news desk of the local station. Television today is loaded with public affairs shows, panel discussions, and documentaries, all designed to provide information or instructional material for their viewers. Whereas TV producers were once reluctant to mention commercial names on the air, they no longer have any timidity about this. Spokesmen and women, paid to advocate products and services, are constantly appearing on talk shows.

The use of a spokesperson can be a most effective tactic. But it can also backfire unless certain guidelines are observed. In placing publicity in the media—particularly through a spokesperson—I always keep in mind that women dominate many markets as readers, television watchers, and consumers. Moreover, they are the big spenders. They're the ones who buy the products for the household, including most of the things related to children. They also buy clothing for themselves and the men in their lives, whose purchases they frequently influence. Every magazine editor is looking for material that tells women readers how to do something better, how to do it more effectively, how to do it more economically. If you can insert your public relations message inoffensively into the framework of this service context, you will be successful with the editor— and your client.

The art of a public relations consultant is to make a client's message fascinating by wrapping it in a presentation that does not suggest advertising or merchandising but entertainment or educational information. Not long ago we placed a client of ours, an optometrist, on the *Today* show. He wasn't there to do a hard-sell job peddling eyeglasses; he was there to talk about the proper toys to be selected by a mother for her children. He pointed out that certain toys enhanced the development of a child's vision. He showed his examples—pogo sticks and electronic games. Along with the optometrist, we put a child on the show who, while the optometrist was speaking, sat on the floor playing, fitting pegs into holes and so forth. Through this low-key selling strategy, the optometrist very effectively got across the message of the American Optometric Association, our client. You, the reader, may be far removed from the corporate business world. And yet you too may have the potential to become a spokesperson by promoting your own credibility before an audience. I'll give an example. Colgate Palmolive brought out a new dental rinse aimed at reducing cavities in young children. It planned to sell this product to mothers and homemakers in their twenties. We recruited for Colgate the past president of the American Woman's Dental Association who was herself the mother of a little girl and was a dentist. My firm trained her and coached her in giving interviews that were subsequently quoted in articles we prepared and placed in magazines. We had selected this woman as the spokesperson for our client because she tied in very much with our client's marketing thrust.

We search the country continually to find suitable spokespeople for our clients. (Who knows? Any one of the readers of this book could turn out to be a qualified candidate for us.) We told one of our clients, the manufacturers of Hanes' Little Boys' Underwear, that we believed he should have a spokesperson for his promotional campaign and he agreed. We decided that our spokesperson should be a child psychologist, preferably someone who had written a book on the subject. The woman we came up with exceeded our expectations. She was not only a child psychologist who was the author of a book, but she had three young children of her own, one a little boy in the right age group for the product.

We put this spokesperson on numerous shows to talk about the problems and challenges of raising young children. In the course of her talk she managed to get in a credit for Hanes' underwear. We placed her on a Christmas program to discuss an offbeat concept. We suggested to her that the subject of her talk be "How does a Jewish child cope with the Christmas holiday in a Christian world?" Does the child feel left out? Does he feel alien and alone? Our spokeswoman observed that although Jewish children are in the minority, there are many things a parent can do to help them be more comfortable. One of the ways, she observed, was to give presents on Christmas day just as Christian parents do. The presents do not have to be on the scale of a color television set or a new computer. They can be much more modest, provided they are given with love. For example—our spokeswoman observed—"children's underwear makes an ideal gift for children." Here was a low-key, but effective, way of promoting our client's product.

What about celebrities as spokespersons? This is an area that PR professionals have been watching closely. The rules of the game are changing. Television is taking a harder line about the use (and misuse) of big names. Paul Noble, the producer of Metromedia's Channel 5 stations in New York, puts it bluntly. "Celebrities are being placed on television for increasingly frivolous reasons. In the old days, for a celebrity to appear on a TV program, he or she had to be there for cause." The cause might be charity, it might be self interest, i.e., the publication of a book or the appearance in a new movie or play, but there was always a professional reason for the appearance. "Now," says Noble, "a celebrity often gets on for no reason whatsoever." This makes life much easier for a PR practitioner. He doesn't have to find anything newsworthy for the celebrity to say.

And there is another development. Due to today's permissiveness, celebrities willingly strip themselves of their privacy and exhibit themselves in all their psychic nakedness. They volunteer stories of children born out of wedlock or of sleeping with the well-known Mr. or Ms. X.

A demythification of celebrities is also taking place; as their privacy is stripped away they are becoming more humanized. In earlier, less openly permissive days, Broadway and Hollywood producers tried to keep their stars away from the public.

When they stayed at a fancy hotel, their PR advisor wouldn't allow them to step into an elevator because if rank-and-file Americans started rubbing shoulders with them, the mystique that surrounded them and was the source of their glamour (the producers believed) would dissolve. By contrast, today's stars frequently indulge in increasingly flagrant exposure to maintain their popularity.

Accompanying the demythification process is a new note of cynicism and irreverence among newspaper journalists and television reporters. Reporters of a generation ago accorded political leaders and other eminent Americans far more respect than today's reporters do. It would have been unthinkable for reporters to deal with Dwight Eisenhower as irreverently as they dealt with Jimmy Carter.

The skepticism, irreverence, and downright contempt with which well-known people are often handled on TV make it a lot trickier and more risky to use celebrity spokespersons than it used to be.

CHAPTER SEVENTEEN

THE
PRESS
CONFERENCE

No one who lives in America is unfamiliar with the press conference. The best-known ones are those held by Presidents of the United States, mayors of large cities, and political luminaries generally. One rule of thumb applies to all press conferences, regardless of who calls them. The more important you are, the more likely it is you will have a large media attendance. If you are unimportant, forget it.

A press corps is assigned exclusively to cover the President of the United States. When the presidential press secretary sends out a notice that the president will hold a press conference, there's not an empty seat in the house. The president always makes news because whatever he says affects some of us in one way or another. Despite the complexities of the job, it is easier to be press secretary to the President of the United States than it is to be press secretary for Joe's Luncheonette. Practically all Joe can talk about is his luncheonette. But the President of the United States can talk about pressing a button to start a nuclear war. This difference does not go unnoticed by the press.

I have conducted countless press conferences. They have ranged from introducing new consumer products to announcing a major lawsuit against the United States Department of Justice. Since I have many capable colleagues out there in the public relations world representing many products, causes, and situations, it can safely be said that in each major city across the United States during the course of any one business day there are hundreds of press conferences, each seeking the full attention of print and broadcast media. Many clients love to be caught up in the excitement of a press conference. Many companies love to hold press conferences because it makes them feel important—whether or not their "news" is important to anyone else. When you're the President of the United States, you can call a press conference to announce whatever you damn please. When you're one of hundreds of thousands of American business corporations, you don't have that latitude.

So when I counsel clients and discuss the possibility of holding a press conference, my rule of thumb is: *if you can't demonstrate it visually, don't hold a press conference.* Press conferences should be used only when there is a significant and dramatic story to tell that requires in-person communication between the storyteller and the media. In the world of business such developments may include new products, mergers and acquisitions, research and development breakthroughs, the appointment of new top management, and the handling of bad news. (We'll cover bad news in another chapter.)

Press conferences can flop in three ways: One, they're boring; two, only three people show up, and two of them are your aunt and uncle; and three, the media don't quite agree with your assessment that significant news is being made and you wind up with absolutely no coverage at all.

I discourage both my own people and our clients from holding press conferences if, in my gut, I feel they are unwarranted. Since I regard the role of public relations as being an arbiter of the news, if no significant news exists, a company is much better off issuing a straightforward press release and hoping it will get some pickup here and there across the country. It is extremely embarrassing and damaging to a public relations agency to hold a press conference for a client when the agency knows in its heart that the media will not be interested.

Those corporate executives who hold infrequent press conferences at which they always make major news announcements play to a packed house. In other cases, however, it's like the boy who cried "wolf." Where an executive and his company hold press conferences fairly frequently to announce dull news, you practically have to pull people in off the streets to fill the room. Unfortunately, a crowd amassed this way doesn't deliver media attention.

When David J. Mahoney called a press conference, the press would always come out in droves. He was a well-known marketing executive who during his career was president of Good Humor Ice Cream, president of Canada Dry, and president of Norton-Simon Inc., the giant consumer products conglomerate. It seemed that Mahoney was always creating new products to receive as much media attention for his company as possible. Some years ago, when he was president of Canada Dry, I was involved in running a press conference for him to announce a major new breakthrough in the soft drink industry—a caffeine-free cola drink to be called "Sport Cola." A press conference was the perfect vehicle to introduce this new product. Before a packed house, Mahoney demonstrated with charts how much caffeine there is in traditional cola drinks. He pointed out that Sport Cola was 99 percent caffeine-free and was going to carve out a major niche in the cola market. As a result of the press conference, Mahoney's picture was on the cover of *Business Week*. Major articles about him and the new product appeared in most of the important business and financial magazines. Unfortunately, Sport Cola never quite made it in the marketplace, but Mahoney got the necessary personal recognition for bigger and better future assignments.

Achieving a successful press conference depends not only on your news and your skills as a persuader but also on luck. All of us who practice public relations pray to the god of timing just before a press conference. We ask the god of timing to be kind to us and not permit any other major news to break during the day of the conference. There is nothing so disastrous for the success of your press conference as another major news story breaking at the same time that will cause the media to absent themselves.

In 1968 I worked on a press conference that had taken months to plan. It involved a Hollywood star who was going to lend her name to a new line of clothing. We planned a dazzling fashion show, coupled with a complicated and dramatic audiovisual presentation. Everything was in order, the media had responded well, and it appeared we were going to have a fine turnout—when the news came over the wire that Robert Kennedy had been shot. Needless to say, the well-laid plans for this entertaining press event went for naught. The press conference was quietly cancelled along with hundreds of others throughout the country that had similarly been planned—for that time.

Conversely, on a "quiet" news day, even the modest news announced at a press conference can achieve surprising media visibility. This is the extraordinary aspect of public relations that can elate as well as deflate practitioners and their clients. One simply cannot predict how much attention a news conference or a news event will receive. As we've discussed, when the President of the United States calls a press conference he can generally count on page one in any newspaper across the country. But when you're the marketing director of XYZ corporation and you're announcing a product to help combat the common cold, you have to hope and pray there are no tidal waves, earthquakes, plane crashes, mass murders, or acts of war to steal your thunder.

Celebrities always help to attract the media. So, as a rule of thumb, if you have a light, non-press-stopping news announcement to make, you might engage the services of a movie star or sports personality. Not too long ago we ran a press conference simply to announce that baseball great Mickey Mantle had been signed on as an advertising spokesperson for a company that helped people with poor credit ratings get credit cards; the place was packed. Mickey Mantle's name alone was able to attract media attendance of well over a hundred people—and the client was beaming.

A major nightmare about holding a press conference is poor attendance. All the preparations are made. Lots of dollars have gone into the renting of a posh facility. Audio-visual presentations have been produced. The client and executives of his company are eagerly awaiting a packed house to convey what they regard as a major breakthrough. After a nervous interval, it becomes clear that two people are sitting in the seats that you have prepared for 50. What to do? What to do?

I can think of few more embarrassing and distressing situations. I remember asking one of our account executives, three days before a client press conference, how many members of the media had committed themselves to being at the press conference. When he told me three, I nearly fainted.

"Are you telling me that three days before a press conference you have only been able to get three reporters to attend?" I screamed. "Calm dowm," he said. "We're going to be on the phone for each of the next three days calling the media. We're bound to get more."

I felt he was overly casual. I suggested that the consequences might be dire if we could not produce at least 20 solid members of the media. I told him he'd better go about the task of producing media people as though our lives depended on it. I asked him that if his life literally depended on our making this press conference a success what would he do? He paused a moment, thought about it, and said, "You know, I never thought about it quite that way before."

I asked him if he was willing to accept the consequences of failure. He told me that he thought the significance of the news to be discussed at the press conference was sufficient motivation for a decent press turnout.

I told him to think about it some more and report back to me in an hour on the steps he would have to take to produce a successful press turnout—if his life depended on it. He left my office deep in thought and, sure enough, an hour later he returned with 10 steps that he and his staff could take to insure a press turnout of substance. They were meaningful recommendations and I agreed they should be carried out. As he was leaving my office, I stopped him for a moment and said, "Arnie, I think you're going to be a great deal more successful in this field if you run every activity as though your life depended on it." He nodded and my point was made.

There is no room in this aspect of the practice of effective public relations for anything but a well-thought-out, well-conceived and well-attended press conference. I simply will not accept a poorly attended press conference. If a press conference is to be recommended and it is in order, then it must be well-attended. And that means being as persuasive as we possibly can in convincing the media that our press conference is significant and worth attending.

One of the facts of life in the public relations field is that once you have run a well-conceived and significant press conference, the media will follow you on to the next one, and the next one, and the one after that. Sometimes we use what we call an editor's workshop as opposed to a press conference. An editor's workshop is a technique which gets editors to do something with their hands. Instead of merely describing a new product and demonstrating it to editors, we actually have editors use the product themselves under the supervision of company personnel. For example, when we introduced some new Singer sewing appliances, we had the editors sewing buttons on, mending rips, and knitting sweaters. For Nestle we taught editors all about coffee beans and how to taste different brands of coffee. And for Schweppes, we had editors mix their own drinks.

We like editors to have fun as well as learn about new products.

CHAPTER EIGHTEEN

HOW TO
GIVE A
"GOOD
INTERVIEW"

As a company attains visibility in the media, journalists will seek interviews with its key people. Too often we tend to view such face-to-face meetings with anxiety when they should be regarded as opportunities to project a positive impression of the company, its products and services, and its contributions.

Here are some guidelines for press interviews which we give our clients.

Basically, there are two circumstances in which officers of a company would be exposed to press interviews: a. The interview is requested by the reporter or editor; or b. the interview is arranged by a public relations representative of the company.

In the first instance, the request for an interview may be prompted by a breaking news story involving the company or its industry. The request for an interview can also be made if the writer is working on a feature story about the industry, the company's area of expertise, or the company itself.

If the interview is requested by the publication, follow these steps:

1. Get the name of the reporter and his publication.

2. Ask for the specific reasons the interview is requested and how much time will be needed.

3. Ask the reporter how he plans to use the interview—strictly as background, as part of a general article on the subject in which other firms will also be quoted, or as the basis for an entire article.

4. Do not respond to questions asked over the telephone. Refer the reporter to the public relations department of the company or the company's public relations firm. Advise them of the request for an interview and the areas that the reporter wishes to cover. Except in the case of a breaking news story, there is usually sufficient time between the request and the actual interview for proper preparation.

Regardless of how an interview originates, it should be regarded as a very serious undertaking. You should enter an interview situation with the assumption that what you say will be seen by thousands of readers. Therefore, you should know in advance not only what you want to say, but how you should express it.

Do not go into an interview situation without thorough preparation—even when you're familiar with the subjects being discussed. Many reporters are extremely knowledgeable about business and financial matters, and will recognize the difference between a top-of-the-head response to a question and a response that has been carefully researched.

Review the subject with others in the company, keeping in mind that the press is looking for something new and/or different. If you have questions, or reservations, do not hesitate to express them. But try to raise these questions far enough in advance so that answers can be obtained before the interview.

Determine the major points you would like to see published in the resulting article and outline them on a sheet of paper. Do not hestitate to have the outline with you at the interview. There is a good chance you can provide the reporter with some supplementary material that will provide greater insights into or understanding of the subject. Prepare such material in advance, refer to it during the interview, and offer it to the interviewer.

Before the interview, obtain several recent issues of the publication and read them carefully to determine how they have handled similar stories, if any, and the type of reader they seem to have been written for. Familiarize yourself with the type of stories the interviewer has written by making a special effort to obtain those issues in which he has stories. Besides giving you a clue as to how he will approach your subject, the fact that you are familiar with his work will flatter him.

Rehearse the interview with someone who plays the role of reporter. Properly conducted, the rehearsal will uncover gaps in information, missing documents, and uncertainties as to the approach to take. On the positive side, it will reinforce your familiarity with the subject matter, give you direction on how to express yourself best, and alert you to potential trouble areas to be avoided.

You may occasionally encounter a reporter who is totally without knowledge or understanding of the subject. This can happen when the business reporter is unavailable and someone from another department is thrown into the breach. In that case, be patient, clear, and simple. At the conclusion of the interview, ask if it would be possible to review the article from a technical viewpoint. In extremely rare instances, if it appears that the reporter's lack of understanding of the subject would result in a grossly inaccurate story, it may be necessary to terminate the interview. In that case, it should be done gracefully.

Unless the interview is held over lunch, try to have it conducted on your own home ground, in your office or conference room. In any case, try to avoid distractions. Hold your telephone calls. Close the office door, and make sure that persons not involved in the interview do not come into the office during that period.

The Interview Itself

The following guidelines generally apply in every interview situation:

1. If you don't want to see it in print, or hear it on the radio or television, *do not say it.* Speaking "off the record" will not insure that the statement will not be used. If the reporter goes to the trouble of getting the same information from another source, after you have provided the lead "off the record," he will be ethically able to use it.

2. Be responsive. Get to the point quickly. It may be sound practice in presentations and written reports to build to your conclusion point by point, but the key to a good interview is in providing direct answers to questions. To do otherwise is to risk boring the reporter so that he misses the point when it is finally made. Furthermore, stating your conclusion early helps to direct the interview your way and can lead to the incorporation of significant details into the story.

3. You may encounter a reporter whose questions appear to be antagonistic. Remain calm and dispassionate. Don't be critical of the reporter or discourteous. Remember that the reporter has a job to do—and in any case, he has the last word.

4. Be open and forthright. Make your responses pertinent and do not evade. If you cannot answer the question for any reason, say so and tell the

reporter why. If you don't know the answer say
you will get it, if possible, and relay it to him.

5. Try to keep your answers short, unless you are
replying to a technical question from a technically
oriented reporter.

6. Use examples whenever you can to illustrate your
point. They not only enliven the story, but will
often influence an editor to give a story much
more prominence than he otherwise would.

7. Don't let a reporter put words into your mouth
unless you agree with the question. Do not repeat
the reporter's terminology, because what you are
doing is making his quote your quote.

8. Do not feel that you have to accept a reporter's
facts or figures. If you disagree, tell him so
politely, and why. If you are not sure, you might
say, "That doesn't seem right to me," and ask for
time to check the data for yourself. Then, make
sure either you or your public relations
representative gets back to the reporter with the
answer.

9. If you consider a question to be inappropriate, you
do not have to answer it. The reporter may try to
generate controversy by drawing you into
evaluations of competitors. You should be
interested in projecting your own expertise, not in
denigrating others.

There are abundant horror stories of luminaries speaking off
the record to reporters only to find their remarks prominently
featured in the next day's newspapers. Secretary of Agriculture
Earl Butz was forced to resign partly because of an intemperate
minority-oriented joke he told off the record to some reporters
traveling with him.

Billy Martin, the former New York Yankee manager, was
fired when in a fit of pique he made disparaging remarks about

George Steinbrenner, the Yankee owner, and Reggie Jackson, who at that time was the star rightfielder. His remarks were also made off the record.

I once arranged an interview of a chief executive officer of an airline company by a business writer for a major New York City newspaper. The executive, a dashing middle-aged man, fancied himself God's gift to women. I knew the reporter was a young woman and cautioned the executive to conduct himself in a professional, businesslike manner.

It was not to be. As soon as the executive saw that the reporter was an attractive young woman, he began to play the role of dandy rather than behave as a business executive. He cooed, winked, and double entendred. His dishonorable intentions were not lost on the reporter. The more she tried to stick to business, the more the executive attempted to sweep her off her feet. I could see a disaster in the making.

To heighten her interest, he began to tell her things off the record—about new air routes, competitive pricing wars, views about the company's competitors, and opinions of managers in his own company. He continued to wink at her as though he had his foot in his eye. Every time I tried to steer him away from divulging classified information, he would preen and say, "Well, she knows this is all by way of background information and off the record."

When the interview ended with the executive inviting the reporter to spend a weekend with him in Bermuda, I left the office with her. Before I had a chance to speak she said, "I know what you're going to say, Art, but I absolutely cannot keep his comments off the record. I never agreed to it, I don't like him, and I'm in a hurry. Good-bye."

Fortunately for me, I had a business trip the following day, because I'm told the roar that filled the corridors when the reporter's story was placed in front of the executive shattered 17 light bulbs.

When you're on television it's even more important to remember that the interviewer is a professional. Barbara Walters is known as one of TV's most effective interviewers. Tex McCrary first coached her in interviewing technique, and she got her training interviewing guests on his TV show. McCrary used to have a training session for his staff which he called the "couch questions" class. Each of his reporters would have to come up every week with one "couch question"—the kind of question that would unfreeze the guest and lure him into revealing himself. Tex taught Walters and Safire how to soften up the interviewee. The first questions would be easy ones, but they would grow harder and harder until the final question fired at the interviewee was the one question he didn't want to answer. The question was, "What is the one thing you don't want to be asked about?" This question invariably provided fascinating disclosures on the show.

To this day Barbara Walters follows the basic strategy laid down by McCrary. She conducts herself with the consummate skill of a public relations practitioner turned journalist. The first couple of questions are designed to relax her guest. From the third question on she builds a sense of urgency and finally delivers the knockout punch. The last question is designed so that the guest, in answering it, will distill "just about everything there is to him or her." This is what Tex McCrary likes to call the "Bartlett's Quotation Question."

The best interview subject is one who does not try to engage in a battle of wits with the interviewer, or to appear superior or clever. Be honest, be straightforward, say what you have to say. That's what it takes.

*T*ex McCrary, shown here with his former wife Jinx Falkenberg, is credited with helping to shape the practice of modern public relations. An advisor to U.S. Presidents, McCrary was instrumental in convincing Dwight Eisenhower to seek the nation's highest office.

CHAPTER NINETEEN

SPECIAL EVENTS: GETTING THE ATTENTION OF THE MARKET

The special event is designed for media attention. It provides opportunities for interesting words and pictures. If it is a well-planned and entertaining event, the media will be glad to give prominence to the client's message while featuring the goings-on.

Our firm deals with a broad spectrum of corporations and institutions—and they all ask us for more and more special-event ideas. It seems as if every time we come back from a client meeting, we convene the troops and grapple with such challenges as how to create a special event to reach, say, chocolate-lovers for Nestle, up-scale audiences for Schweppes, or bewildered males for Singer sewing machines.

My staff responds to these challenges, sometimes with "off-the-wall" ideas—a women's wrestling event in melted chocolate; an underwater extravaganza in Schweppes tonic water; a Singer rip-your-clothes-off festival.

In brainstorming sessions the first ideas are not necessarily the best, but they pave the way for the good ones that follow. The point is there has been a major shift in the services that public relations provides. At one time we were engaged in traditional product publicity and the occasional press-agent stunt to generate media attention. Today the stunt has evolved into the event—a much more sophisticated tool.

As one who's been around the public relations field awhile, I am delighted to see this trend. So many wonderful ideas come out of it that benefit everyone. Special events generally serve the public as well as the sponsors. Over the next few years, this type promotion will be the fastest-growing segment of corporate campaigns.

Special-events promotions are moving rapidly into new areas of public interest and concern. Companies will be looking for, and devising, different kinds of special events beyond the narrow confines of sports and music.

As such, special events promotions are becoming more versatile, and demonstrate an increasing capacity to stabilize product markets. Promotion costs are becoming competitive with advertising and various approaches to discount offers, whether to distributors, retailers, or the public.

The public is getting involved in the creative aspects of special events. They are becoming more sophisticated participants. Community groups are learning how to combine their interests with those of the promoter of a product or service. This is one of the key elements in special-events promotion.

"Brandstanding," a term I coined to describe a technique that promotes products by linking them to events and issues of interest to consumers, will grow rapidly because advertising costs will continue to rise. We are approaching the era of the million-dollar network minute. There are many products for which companies cannot finance television advertising, but that can show good profits if kept in the public eye. Such products can achieve visibility through brandstanding.

New-product publicity, of course, concentrates on product characteristics. For a great many products, the time comes when it is difficult to generate effective publicity. Although the product is well-known, customers may want to try something new and different. At that point it becomes important to keep the public aware of your product.

That's where brandstanding and special-events promotion provide great leverage. Linking a tried-and-true product—or product line—to an event, issue, or idea creates for the item or brand name an aura of excitement, interest, reliability, and renewed vitality.

Lobsenz-Stevens surveyed 200 marketing directors and brand managers. We asked them to rate methods for improving sales of an already well-known product. Of five methods, finding a new market segment rated first. New advertising campaigns and product improvement ran neck-and-neck for second place, but trailed far behind the preferred method. New packaging placed fourth.

The single most important finding of the study, however, was that 76 percent of those surveyed expected to use special events to help market their products at some future time. The respondents were well-known consumer product companies.

Many practitioners recognize the potential of special-event promotions. What is needed is innovative public relations thinking. There is a limit to how effective a campaign can be if it is simply a copy of what has already been done. The promotion value declines.

When special events are used imaginatively, they can produce remarkable results—results that transcend other forms of promotion. Because they capture the imagination of the media, special events generate extraordinary coverage.

Let's look at some of the benefits of new special-event ideas for marketing:

- Each idea can be tested just as you test-market new products. The idea can be used for a limited local campaign, to bolster local marketing thrusts, or it can be broadened for regional or national promotions.

- New ideas can focus on precise, selected demographic segments of the public, and can be as selective as advertising.

- The concepts can carry almost any kind of message about the products, service, or brand line. In fact, they can communicate about your product as no other approach can.

- Innovative special events can create long-term visibility because such campaigns can be repeated after a lapse or become ongoing promotions.

- Special events can be integrated into other promotion efforts, such as advertising, to enhance the effectiveness of all elements in a marketing campaign.

- Special events generate far more media attention than other forms of product or brand publicity.

- The cost-effectiveness of this tool often exceeds other forms of promotion.

It is important for those who create sponsored programs to look beyond sports and music. This is not to say that we've reached the saturation point in sports and music, but that we may simply be limiting our thinking.

Colgate-Palmolive's creative sports program promotes school competitions in most of the 60 countries in which it does business. Each competition is treated as a local event. New York's contest is "The Colgate Women's Games."

The program has a strong community service orientation. It is conducted among college-age women in New York City and Jersey City, New Jersey, and consists of a series of track-and-field events involving some 20,000 competitors. The finals are held in Madison Square Garden. For the last several years they have been the subject of an hour-long special on ABC-TV.

Colgate does not view the games as strictly product promotion. They represent a Colgate commitment to return something to the communities in which the company does business. And this attitude is becoming more characteristic of special-events promotions. The company's name, however, appears in school newspapers, community newspapers, sports pages, TV listings and reviews, and is mentioned on TV news shows.

Hertz uses a brandstanding campaign that is integrated with its advertising and other marketing efforts, linking the campaign with the Hertz slogan, "We're Number One." The program is a sports event, but with a difference. Local sports writers across the nation are asked to pick the top high school athletic performance of the year in each of the 50 states.

The process culminates in a banquet at which Hertz spokesman O. J. Simpson makes "Number One" presentations to the athletes selected. Newspapers, radio, and TV cover the event, and Mr. Simpson has appeared on *Good Morning, America* for the past three years when the athletes convene in New York.

Coverage of related events often results in added publicity. For example, when Martina Navratilova lost the Avon championship in 1982, UPI issued a story that said she could console herself because her chances for the million-dollar Playtex prize were still good. And after she won three of the four "Playtex Challenge" tournaments, the company got extraordinary media exposure.

Following are six essential characteristics of the effective special event.

1. It has publicity value in its own right. If the event is not of interest, neither the media nor the public will respond.

2. It provides the desired positioning. It must be of intrinsic interest to potential customers—customers who will buy, and buy again.

3. It is linked meaningfully to the product or brand name. For example, "The Playtex Challenge" links the Playtex name to women's pursuit of excellence, fitness, and health.

4. It is run smoothly so that the product link is effective but not intrusive. The program should be interesting, exciting, and meaningful to the public whether or not your name is associated.

5. It is communicated to the public and media through an effective promotion campaign. Special-events promotion should be viewed as focused marketing tools.

6. It is innovative. Create your own events. Create something you can own. Listen to others' ideas for events that haven't been done before.

An examination of several examples illustrates how varied the special-events technique really is. By shifting our thinking from traditional sports and music sponsorships to other areas, we can create effective promotions well-suited to specific objectives.

A conservation issue—saving the American bald eagle—serves as a platform for promoting Eagle Rare Bourbon. The distiller has developed a brochure on the eagle and an information clearing house works closely with wildlife specialists, and helps operate emergency centers that treat injured birds and return them to the wild. Media coverage mentions Eagle Rare Bourbon.

Clairol has a successful program that links an art exhibit of mother-and-child paintings to hair-care products. On tour for many years, the exhibit generates good publicity and draws large crowds. Many of the viewers, of course, are potential Clairol customers.

Other areas with general appeal include safety campaigns, promotions involving special awards, and health fairs. The Metropolitan Life Insurance Company, for example, has made good use of a series of health fairs—the company has organized close to 30 such fairs in the New York area alone. They featured booths manned by volunteer health professionals qualified to provide helpful health and medical information. Local media coverage was extensive, from community newspapers to network TV news.

An event held last year in Washington, D.C.'s Rock Creek Park offers another good illustration. Called "Everybody's Bike Day," it was sponsored by the Bicycle Federation in cooperation with the Bicycle Manufacturers Association, American Youth Hostels, and six other organizations.

In addition to bicycle-riding over a route closed to traffic, the activity featured a parade, appearances by celebrities (including Olympic athletes), picnics, a rock group, unicycling and tumbling demonstrations, and a contest for bicycle tire-changing. It also offered clinics on safety, bicycle adjustment and selection, and repairs and maintenance. In short, virtually everything a biker might be interested in.

The event provided a basis to promote local bicycling clubs and other membership organizations interested in fitness and health. Exhibitors and sponsors included companies and organizations with products and services aimed at the fitness- and sports-conscious. Also participating were commercial organizations directly involved with products and services related to biking activities.

In all, some 32 organizations participated or exhibited at the event, including the Washington, D.C. Police Department, which registered bicycles for their owners, the Environmental Protection Agency, the D.C. Transportation Authority, and the D.C. Department of Recreation.

The event was well attended, extensively publicized in advance, and well covered by the media. It created exactly the kind of opportunity to reach a selected audience that is the mark of a successful special event promotion.

CHAPTER TWENTY

DAMAGE
CONTROL:
HOW TO
HANDLE
BAD NEWS

The ultimate test of PR professionals may be their coolness, decisiveness, and skill in dealing with adverse events that have the power to destroy an enterprise and create havoc in thousands of lives.

In December 1984 the world was shocked to learn that more than 2,000 Indians had died as a result of the accidental discharge of toxic chemicals from a Union Carbide plant at Bhopal, India, 350 miles south of New Delhi. Though this catastrophe was one of the worst industrial accidents in history, it was typical of those that happen every day on a smaller scale— fires, plane crashes, environmental disasters, product failures, sabotage.

In dealing with such grim events, it is not the role of the PR professional to minimize the accident or its consequences but rather to get the news out honestly and help corporate people know what to do when the company is suddenly besieged by reporters. When the calamity is of major proportions, it not only attracts the media of the world, it acts as a magnet for casualty lawyers. Within days of the Bhopal disaster celebrated attorney Melvin Belli announced he was bringing a $15 billion suit against Union Carbide on behalf of all those affected.

This is the acid test for a company—not just for its public relations department but for its guts and character. It is noteworthy that, right after the Union Carbide catastrophe, the company's board chairman flew to India. He was risking his life—he was in fact arrested—but he wanted to demonstrate Union Carbide's commitment and its immediate willingness to assume responsibility.

Corporate public relations professionals have contingency plans for such occurrences. Not long ago seven people were poisoned in the Chicago area after taking Extra Strength Tylenol, a product sold by a subsidiary of Johnson & Johnson (J & J).Someone had put cyanide into the Tylenol capsules. Disclosure of this threatened a nationwide panic. But what could have become a disaster with far-reaching implications for the U.S. pharmaceutical industry, was avoided.

J & J was saved by the clear-headed, candid, and thoroughly professional behavior of its public relations people in its hour of crisis.

The news first reached Lawrence Foster, the company's vice president of public relations, via a phone call from a Chicago reporter. Foster and his staff, and the management of J & J which supported him, made a quick decision to place public concern ahead of private interest. Foster's goal was not to whitewash anything but to get at the truth. At first he had no idea of the magnitude of the problem and the challenge he had to deal with. He did not know whether the Tylenol bottles that were poisoned were contaminated in the actual manufacturing process of J & J, so before issuing a defensive statement to the press, he sent one of his staff by plane to Chicago where the poisonings had taken place. He assigned 50 people from the corporate family to handle banks of telephones and answer the more than 1,000 calls from the press that were to come in over the next week.

Fortunately the lines of communication through J & J's top management made for swift, effective action. Foster had direct access to James Burke, the chairman, and was in the habit of walking into Burke's office or phoning him without having to go through channels.

There were some delicate decisions to make, and some formidable hurdles to overcome. All Tylenol bottles in the Chicago area were immediately recalled from the drugstores. Foster and his staff hotly debated to what extent if at all the American public realized that it was Johnson & Johnson that operated the subsidiary firm which manufactured Tylenol. J & J was doing a multimillion dollar business with a host of other products, and J & J management wanted to know the extent to which the Tylenol disaster could impair its image with the American consumer, affecting sales for its other lines. In an effort to learn the answer, Foster asked the staff of a television studio (operated by the corporation) to monitor every newscast around the country that mentioned Tylenol over the next 10 days. This monitoring confirmed what Foster himself suspected—the American public *did* associate Tylenol with J & J.

From then on, the expert handling of public relations virtually saved Tylenol from extinction. Conscious that the public welfare was the top priority and that the press could be an ally rather than an adversary, the J & J people candidly warned the public of the danger, at the same time doing their best to prevent the panic from spreading by putting the crisis in its proper perspective. Responsible reporting by the news media played a fundamental role, but underlying this was the fact that Johnson & Johnson told everything it knew about what was happening and promptly took steps to safeguard the public by developing new triple-seal packaging. In frankly presenting its case, J & J replied to several thousand media inquiries.

Research indicated that although over 90 percent of the public knew about the Tylenol poisonings, thanks to the fact that J & J was up front in disclosing the facts as they were without distortion, the public became convinced that J & J and Tylenol were as much the victims of the tragedy as the unfortunate consumers.

By taking the advice of its public relations staff, J & J's management saved the day. Had the company's public relations people panicked and handled the matter differently, they might well have triggered a nationwide backlash against the pharmaceutical business. The ensuing public and legislative uproar might in turn have led to increased government regulation, effectively shackling the industry. But because of the way the company handled its public relations, no such backlash occurred. The product returned with new safety packaging and the crisis was over.

Jim Burke, the chairman of J & J, called a press conference a year after the Tylenol experience to review what had happened. "I suspect no story has ever been told as quickly and as clearly—with as little confusion—as this one," he said. Tylenol not only survived but recovered its top market position.

When a company faces a major problem, the stakes are high. Sometimes, as in the Tylenol case, the matter is one of survival; many firms do not make it. In one such case, a firm that marketed a line of gourmet soups under the Bon Vivant label was charged with putting out a tainted product that caused several deaths. The company was forced out of business.

Consumer goods companies face not only the constant possibility of real accidents and failures, but the possibility of sabotage, as in the Tylenol case, and the everyday reality of threats and blackmail. Ken Defren, a senior public relations executive at General Foods, observes that his company and others like it are frequently contacted by deranged people who threaten to poison food products on the supermarket shelves unless they are paid ransom.

The companies must have contingency public relations plans to handle bad news of all sorts, and maintain security divisions to look into each threat, no matter how bizarre. All such threats are taken seriously; none can be ignored. The effort to investigate the threat and the effort to avoid alarming the public proceed on parallel paths.

The blundering misuse of public relations in the case of Three Mile Island nuclear plant disaster set back the entire nuclear energy industry. When the accident occurred at Three Mile Island, the utility company did not handle the media well. It failed to make itself available; it gave distorted facts; it did not mobilize public opinion properly. Newspaper reporters at the scene complained they were being misled by the conflicting statements that emanated from corporate sources. The nuclear accident occurred at four o'clock in the morning. The company did not notify civil defense agencies until more than three hours later. It refused to admit there had been a radiation accident until three hours after that. Spokesmen told different stories to different news reporters.

As a result of mishandling the story, public opinion turned sharply against the nuclear power industry. Ordinary middle-class Americans who had never before joined a dissent movement united with antinuclear militants in opposing nuclear power. This mainstream opinion, which turned against the industry, provided a new respectability for the entire antinuclear movement.

The public backlash has now reached the courts. Indictments have been handed up against other nuclear power stations. The impact of mishandled public relations and the damage to the industry's image have been far-reaching, and the repercussions continue.

Every organization faces the possibility of having to deal with the potentially negative consequences of such bad news. Whether the circumstances attract international attention, as happened with Three Mile Island, or capture only local interest, the effects of bad news can cause significant and lasting problems. Which means that every organization needs policy guidelines and an action plan for dealing with bad news.

Media people swarm over such stories, hungry to obtain and disseminate news of broad human interest. They reach so many people so quickly their impact on public attitudes toward a corporation or its products can be deep and lasting. The era when a Vanderbilt could say "The public be damned" is gone. Today a corporation's health requires good relationships with its many publics—its customers, its neighbors, its employee base, its stockholder base, and its suppliers. And how a corporation interacts with the media when bad news happens is increasingly crucial to these relationships.

All too often, when bad news breaks, the corporate image suffers out of proportion to the company's responsibility. This results from media misinterpretation of events rather than accurate assessment. Whatever the cause, review of the news handling process of companies in crisis often indicates questionable judgment and inadequate preparation regarding how best to handle bad news when it occurs.

The public gains a poor impression if it perceives the corporation to be unresponsive, confused, inept, reluctant, or unable to provide reliable information. A defensive posture generates a bad impression.

What most often underlies inadequate handling of bad news is defensiveness regarding the company's scope of activity in an emergency. If a company is uncomfortable about granting permission to legitimately concerned elements of the public to look over its shoulder, examine its premises and processes, and then communicate the findings, that attitude can readily become evident in the handling of news in crisis situations. Under such circumstances results in terms of public opinion are far more likely to prove negative than positive, not only in the short term but also over the long haul.

There is a basic anomaly in dealing with crises—one that often influences how an organization handles crisis news. The primary objectives for dealing with the crisis itself involve minimizing the short-term effects. Whether the emergency involves death, injury, or damage, the principal aim of the emergency team is to bring events under control in a manner that reduces death and injury to the lowest possible level, then limits the physical damage in terms of costs and time needed to restore normal operations. These priorities are clear. They establish the decision-making sequence for emergency crews.

By contrast, the news requires a different orientation. In handling the news, long-term consequences need high priority. Where consumer products are concerned, public confidence in the quality and integrity of those products is essential. The public will accept momentary aberrations, whatever their cause, if it feels assured they are indeed momentary. But if the fundamental credibility of the organization behind the product erodes, the impact on sales becomes a long-term matter. Brand loyalties disappear causing products to vanish.

Dealing with the possibility of having to recall products is an accepted part of life for many manufacturers of consumer products. Major manufacturers of canned foods now have contingency plans to deal with the possibility of product contamination. The primary concern is to get all suspect products off the shelves and out of the distribution process rapidly, if possible overnight. Communicating to the public about the protective actions taken is equally important. Obviously sales and consumption will suffer an instantaneous drop to zero. But maintaining public confidence will enable the product to recapture its share of market. In most cases sales can return to profitable levels in a few weeks and regain most of their former sales vigor inside of six months.

Executives experienced in dealing with bad news believe it is a mistake ever to take a position from which you can be forced to retreat. This runs counter to adversarial thinking, which typifies legal contests and debates, and may cause executives to feel it is a mistake to yield any ground whatsoever.

Jack O'Dwyer, publisher of Jack O'Dwyer's Newsletter, considers the United States government response to the Russian downing of the Korean jetliner that strayed into a Russian air zone to have been ill-advised.

"U.S. government spokespersons were not interested in the facts at the outset. They just shot from the hip and might have come close to getting us into World War Three. It's a classic public relations example of how not to handle bad news. The object is to gather your facts first and *then* make your statements, not the opposite."

Today any hint of "stonewalling" is taken as evidence of a) unconcern for the public good, and b) possible complicity in activities counter to the public interest.

Perhaps not as damning, but potentially equally destructive of public trust, is the appearance of incompetence. Whenever a corporation seems to lack the willingness or the capacity to respond to an emergency, get it under control, and give the media (and thereby the public) an accurate accounting of events and their portent, the corporation allows an aura of ineptness to taint its image. This, too, erodes public trust. The destruction of public faith may spread beyond one specific organization, altering the public perception of whole industries.

Many industries live with the possibility of significant bad news related to public safety or well-being: these include airlines, mining companies, chemical companies, and food manufacturers, among others. In these industries there is a consensus that every sizeable corporation—regardless of its field—needs a working understanding of how to deal with bad news when it happens. On any given day, any of these companies may have to respond to an emergency situation involving bad news.

Their executives know that whenever an emergency arises, media representatives will dig in and get information about events, find people to interview, and obtain interpretations, explanations, and background data. That's their job. So over the years industries that live with the possibility of highly visible emergencies have evolved procedures and guidelines which enable them to minimize the impact of bad news.

How to Proceed

Since media people are going to develop news reports whenever an emergency arises, it makes sense to establish procedures insuring that the media people speak to company representatives who are articulate, fully informed, and capable of stating company policies. To achieve and maintain this level of readiness to respond requires a basic set of emergency procedures such as these:

1. Notify Top Management Immediately.

As soon as an emergency occurs, notify two people. First, someone in the upper echelon who is authorized to take action. Second, someone who will serve as a spokesperson. Both need to be alerted immediately.

This step permits management to mobilize its capacity to deal with both the emergency itself and with the news about the emergency.

It is important for this initial communication to contain all of the information that can be significant at this point. What happened and where are absolute minimums. How many people are affected or threatened, what response measures are being employed, whether the situation is out of control or contained. Any other pertinent information will also help. Such detailed information establishes the company spokesperson from the very beginning of the emergency as the best-informed and most reliable source of information. This encourages the media to develop its coverage using corporation-supplied information.

This procedure is basic with all the industries mentioned. Airlines, for example, notify key people as soon as anything occurs that might develop into risks to passengers or flight personnel. Those key people include an upper-echelon executive and a public relations executive.

Typically, as soon as an emergency arises, chemical companies, petroleum companies, and mining companies also alert a top executive who is authorized to take action, and a spokesperson authorized to keep the media informed.

If the media don't already know about the emergency, it is a good idea for the public relations person to inform them. Let the media recognize that the corporation is actively providing fast, direct, informative, responsible access to the news.

2. Channel Inquiries for Information to the Spokesperson.

Every person on the management staff, from the executives to the firstline supervisors, should refer all requests for information about an emergency to the designated spokesperson. By the same token, any information available to them that might be relevant to reporting or understanding the emergency should also be given to the spokesperson.

In this way one key individual will become the best qualified person to interact with the media. If the media find that person well informed, reliable, and forthcoming, coverage of the story will concentrate on company sources. That is a basic objective, for it will ensure that the media—and the public—have an opportunity to assess the company's policies and point of view.

The appearance of openness is important to maintaining optimum credibility with the media. There are exceptions, however. If giving out information may cause unnecessary anguish to members of the public, it is better to withhold it. Air crashes offer a case in point. Withholding the names of passengers and crew serves to protect families from misinformation, tension-producing speculation, and aggressive intrusion by determined newspeople. There will be a proper time for release of such information. But verification of who was actually on board the flight, determination of their current condition, and communication about the victims with the next of kin should all precede release of their names and addresses.

3. Set up a News Center.

There are two reasons for establishing a specific location where news is made available to the media. First, doing so simplifies delivering reliable information to the media. It serves to improve the efficiency of information gathering, verifying, organizing, and delivery.

Second, locating the news center near, but not at, the crisis scene lowers the confusion level for those dealing with the actual crisis. Their work is not hampered by reporters and camera crews who may get in the way, or by having to divide their attention between crisis events and media people. Until the crisis is under control or has passed the critical phase, the fewer media people at the scene the better. This is not meant to exclude cameramen and their crews who provide visual coverage of news stories. It aims at minimizing crisis-scene confusion.

4. Make Impact Projections.

For companies who seldom experience crisis situations that draw media attention, it is extremely important to have executive-level evaluations of the impact the emergency will have on the company. The ways in which information is presented to the media will affect several aspects of company operations.

Having someone available who can project company-wide effects will often enable the news-response team to reduce those effects. By including elements in the total communication effort that are aimed at reassuring specific segments of the public, the long-term problems can be minimized.

With every crisis, chain-reaction effects are inevitable. A fire, for instance, may have an immediate impact on production schedules, which may later slow deliveries, then depress sales, reduce earnings, and even force readjustment of the debt structure. If the company is aware of this possibility it may be able to include loyalty-enhancing messages to its stockholders at the time of the crisis, thereby lessening the downstream financial impact. But to do so the news-response team must have an awareness of the possible implications, an understanding of stockholder thinking and motivation, and the ability to devise appropriate messages that are relevant to the emergency situation.

The immediate effect of a product-contamination problem may be to erode sales. But long-term effects might include scrutiny by government agencies and/or consumer organizations, revision of production processes, layoffs of production personnel, lowered employee morale and efficiency, and eventually the need for costly new fringe benefits to deal with human resource problems.

Media inquiries can be handled in a way that addresses many potential future problems. Emphasis can be given to the company's compliance with governmental and consumer standards. Discussion of the causes can be cast in language that not only avoids allowing any onus to fall on the employees, but actually projects management respect for company personnel and the integrity of their performance.

Companies such as mine operators and airlines, whose people have been through numerous crisis experiences, will probably be able to let the key spokesperson make these projections. This individual may be fully competent to do so. But companies that deal with crises only rarely need to include an experienced general executive on the news response team.

5. Gather a Response Team.

Dealing with the media will usually require the efforts of more than one person. The spokesperson may need people to answer phones, maintain a media-contact log, track crisis events and verify factual information, interpret and analyze technical aspects of the situation, and consider the company-wide implications of unfolding events.

The spokesperson must be authorized to obtain whatever support he or she feels is relevant. And the spokesperson will usually need an assistant to locate and assemble such a media-response group.

6. "Dry Run" Insurance.

Use of dry runs enables a company to maintain an efficient capacity to deal with bad news. Being able to mobilize the response team is fundamental to having an effective response.

Dry runs and simulated emergencies are widely used by companies that may have to deal with a crisis at any moment. Petroleum companies not only check to be sure they can call emergency teams into action, most of them maintain training programs that keep emergency people, including their spokespeople, abreast of current technology in dealing with spills, fires, explosions.

Airlines check their ability to respond to crisis situations as frequently as once a month. Chemical companies engage in crisis alerts in order to maintain the ability to deal with such emergencies as deployment of crews to tank-car spillages involving hazardous chemicals. And all of the industries with crisis experience include instructions and preparations for dealing with the media. They consider it an intrinsic part of their response procedures.

How to Respond

Having a set of procedures for calling a response group into action provides a media response capability. Companies experienced at handling crises follow a set of guidelines to ensure achievement of practical goals. The guidelines can be stated in a few do's and don'ts:

1. Never Speculate.

Engaging in guesswork or speculating about any aspect of the crisis or about company policy is a no-no. All reports to the media must be based on verified facts. If a specialist is needed to explain a technological context, make it absolutely clear that the specialist is providing background, not reporting on the crisis.

2. Be Open.

Withholding information is almost certain to backfire. Reporters are expert at discovering what is going on. And when withheld information comes to light, the company looks as if it were deliberately trying to hide information to cover up some degree of malfeasance.

There are two exceptions: If releasing information might cause unnecessary pain, sit on it. Divulging the name of a victim of a fatality before the family is properly notified is a clear example. The second circumstance in which it is proper to withhold information has to do with exceeding one's authority. Stating the cause of death, for example, is the responsibility of a doctor or a coroner. Another example is reporting the cause of an air crash, which is solely the responsibility of the Air Safety Board. Even if excellent evidence exists, and the media response group is confident it knows the answers to such questions, they should nonetheless be referred to those authorized to make the official determinations.

Avoid appearing to dodge media requests. Maintain a log of all inquiries so that every request can be honored. Avoid "no comment" responses. It is far better to say something like, "We don't have a verifiable answer to your question at this time, but when we do you'll get it." Or, "We're trying to get that information, and we'll give it to you as soon as we have it." Or, "All we know at present is . . . " and spell out what has been verified.

Always convey the impression that your company is working diligently to be the best-informed source of information available and that it is determined to provide reliable, factual coverage.

Provide media access to top executives. In dealing with a serious crisis, it is effective to have a top executive talk to the media. A press briefing is an acceptable forum, but individual interviews can also prove useful. The words of a top executive, especially those of a policy maker, carry more import than the same statement from a professional spokesperson. It is usually well worth the executive's time.

3. Establish and Convey Clear Corporate Policies.
One of the most significant tools available in handling crisis news consists of stating company policies in unambiguous terms. Doing so often prevents or attenuates the development of resentments, fears, anger, and hostility.

4. Allow the Story to Fade Away.
All news stories have a life of their own. It is important to handle bad news while it is live. After it fades from public

view, let it rest in peace. Sometimes companies feel a need to counteract the effects of bad news in a way that resurrects it. Doing so is a mistake. Once it is out of public awareness, it is usually best left alone.

By following these guidelines, a company can interact effectively on a wide range of specific bad-news situations. Using them will enable a company to maintain good rapport with the media and provide a means to protect itself from loss of public good will despite emergency circumstances fraught with potential pitfalls.

Bob Hope entertaining the troops. His annual trek to boost the morale of our "front lines" somewhere in the world was originally engineered by modern-day public relations pro Tex McCrary to help break the Russian blockade of Berlin.

CHAPTER TWENTY ONE

PR:
A POSITIVE
FORCE

The power to persuade, like the power to split the atom, is in itself neither good nor bad. Power can be used to achieve positive goals, or to destroy. The persuasion explosion is happening. The mid-20th century has seen the rise of a new and highly influential discipline. Public relations is a fact of life today. Public relations practitioners are using, and will continue to use, their discipline in a wide range of causes to reach all sorts of goals.

Some of those goals will be universally seen to be beneficial. In many cases the masters of the principles of PR will use their strength to benefit a limited number of people. And it is deplorable but inevitable that PR power misused can and will attain objectives that are, on balance, harmful to society.

What can't be denied is that PR *works*. Even its most virulent and unrelenting critics admit that. And we must remember something that is often overlooked—*public relations is still in its infancy*. This is a very new discipline. It has already demonstrated its potency, but we can expect the strategies and tactics of persuasion to be strengthened and sharpened to a degree that most people cannot even envision right now.

Anything that has as much power as PR is a significant force. Although its major uses today are commercial and political, it has the potential to shape opinion and perception in all areas of society.

This frightens some people. They don't like what public relations can do, so they want it to go away. They try to make it go away by denouncing it. Their efforts have met with the same degree of success as that enjoyed by King Canute in bidding the waves to recede. It's like trying to put toothpaste back in the tube. The genie of PR is out of the bottle, and no amount of denunciation and handwringing can force it back in.

And why should it? The genie is not inherently evil. If we make friends with it, and learn how to use its power, we can do many good things, and some great things.

PR people are "friends of the genie." They understand what persuasion can do, and how the right kind of information, disseminated the right way, can be the most powerful force in the world.

Tex McCrary, who was present at the dawn of modern PR, knows this. He was also present some four decades ago when another immensely powerful genie had just been let out of the bottle. When the first atomic bombs were dropped on Hiroshima and Nagasaki, McCrary was one of the first Western eyewitnesses to the resulting cataclysm.

At the time, McCrary, who was doing PR for the U.S. Air Force, asked the Joint Chiefs of Staff for two B-17 planes and a staff of cameramen and newspapermen to fly with him into Hiroshima and Nagasaki and report on the damage caused by the bombs. He received the planes and the support for what he sensed was to be the biggest story to emerge from the war. Shortly after the bombing, Tex flew into Hiroshima. "The smell of death was overwhelming," he recalls. Sensing that what would confront them might be too painful to be reported to the American public, McCrary did not permit the civilian news correspondents to enter the cities with him. "They did not see, as I saw, the heaps of bodies stacked and still burning five days after the bomb had been dropped. But I did take a photographer from *Life* magazine along. We wrapped our testicles in lead foil because we were fearful of what would happen to us from the atomic radiation. Our testicles were one part that we wanted to save."

As the two Americans walked through the living hell of Hiroshima, McCrary said to his photographer, "Goddamn it, Bernie, I brought you around the world to shoot pictures, so go ahead and shoot." When they finished their tour and left the city McCrary walked over to the reporters who had waited outside and spoke to them. "I do not think that the folks back home will understand what we have seen here."

President Truman had ordered the bomb to be dropped to shorten the war and to save American lives and his motives were understandable. But none of the bomb's developers had foreseen the awesome dimensions of the effects of atomic radiation. McCrary had seen the devastation first hand. "This to me is an atrocity, pure and simple," he told his staff. "We have put two cities to the sword. These were civilian centers filled with old men, women, and children. I don't see how we can run this story back home."

In this arbitrary fashion, McCrary in his capacity as an officer assigned to the U.S. Air Force imposed press censorship. The stories that found their way into the newspapers and magazines were heavily watered down. Only one picture showing the actual devastation wrought by the A bombs appeared in the U.S. The *Life* photographer had snapped a photo of a marble head of Christ that had been erected by Christian missionaries in downtown Hiroshima. "You could see the marble split down the middle from the force of the explosion," Tex recounts. "You saw the face of Christ and you saw the wasteland surrounding it." *Life* magazine ran this picture, the only one to be published at that time by the American press.

The extent of the horror caused by the dropping of the atomic bombs was not revealed to the American public for two years. No newspaper editor or publisher would print the story.

By this time Tex deeply regretted his on-the-spot decision to refuse to allow the civilian news correspondents accompanying him to witness and report on the unprecedented devastation of the two cities. Now he undertook to do whatever he could to get the truth publicized.

One night, at dinner, he met Harold Ross, editor of *The New Yorker*. John Hersey, a correspondent who had managed to get into Hiroshima after Tex had left and written about what he saw, had been trying without success to get his story published. McCrary pitched in to help him. The editor of the magazine, responding to McCrary's urging, replied that he was willing to print Hersey's story. "But as you know, *The New Yorker* does not publish pictures." Ross, however, made a dramatic decision. "I'll tell you what we will do. In order to make the readers fully experience what actually happened, we'll drop all our advertising for one issue and print the story from beginning to end." This was how the American public first learned the true story of the bombing of Hiroshima and Nagasaki.

McCrary understood that people need complete information—the full story—to be able to deal with momentous issues . . . that the direction of information is the heart and soul of persuasion . . . and that informed opinion is the world's best hope in times of tremendous danger.

No PR professional is unaware that there are individuals who have mastered the craft of persuasion in order to aggrandize themselves at the expense of others. As we have pointed out, the principles of PR can be used for bad as well as good.

What defense do we have against this? To me knowledge is the best defense. When we understand how public relations works, and realize the extent to which it has penetrated into all aspects of our lives, we are better equipped to separate the good from the bad.

Beyond this, when people learn to use the power of PR for themselves they need no longer be mere receptors, targets, or pawns. They can instead turn the strengths of the discipline to their own advantage to achieve personal goals. And in the process they become better able to work together to use the power of persuasion to attain their larger goals.

This to me is the best way for society to deal with the power of PR. Let's not try to keep the levers of persuasion in the hands of a select few. Let's make the concepts and the techniques available to everyone, as this book tries to do.

Make no mistake about it. The explosion is taking place. *The genie is here.* Everyday we see ideas we oppose—even hate—being promulgated. In the United States the traditions of a democratic society and the safeguards of the First Amendment protect those ideas. Now we have to get used to the fact that ideas we don't like are not only going to be voiced, they are going to be voiced with all of the persuasive power of a newly developed art of persuasion. There's no question that this will test our traditions and our fidelity to free speech. It's one thing to see a guy on a soapbox ranting about turning the world upside down. He can be dismissed as a crackpot. But when those same "crackpot" ideas are advanced with immense power and subtlety, we're apt to feel profoundly threatened.

Yet society is safe . . . for several reasons. An informed public can be trusted ultimately to make the right decisions. PR professionals, who live with and use the power of persuasion every day, maintain, on the whole, high standards of ethics in exerting that power. This is not because they are saints, but because they understand that it is in their own best interest to do so—and also because they are as concerned as anyone else about what tomorrow will bring for this world we live in. After all, it's the only world we've got. We don't want to blow it up.

The code of professional standards for the practice of public relations set forth by the Public Relations Society of America is unequivocal:

"Members of the Public Relations Society of America base their professional principles on the fundamental value and dignity of the individual, holding that the free exercise of human rights, especially freedom of speech, freedom of assembly and freedom of the press, is essential to the practice of public relations.

"In serving the interests of clients and employers, we dedicate ourselves to the goals of better communication, understanding and cooperation among the diverse individuals, groups and institutions of society, and of equal opportunity of employment in the public relations profession.

"We pledge:

"To conduct ourselves professionally, with truth, accuracy, fairness and responsibility to the public."

In a world increasingly vulnerable to nuclear self-destruction, it may be that the only thing that can save us is the ability to reach out and communicate with our neighbors everywhere to arrive at the understanding that, despite our differences, we have a common interest in survival.

A crucial role in this effort at communication for survival can be played by public relations professionals working with the media to get across the most important message ever promoted—*peace on our planet*—on behalf of its most important client—*the human race.*

Index